W. S. MERWIN

SELECTED TRANSLATIONS 1948-1968

BOOKS BY W. S. MERWIN

POEMS

The Lice   *1967*
The Moving Target   *1963*
The Drunk in the Furnace   *1960*
Green With Beasts   *1956*
The Dancing Bears   *1954*
A Mask for Janus   *1952*

TRANSLATIONS

Selected Translations 1948–1968   *1968*
The Song of Roland   *1963*
Lazarillo de Tormes   *1962*
The Satires of Persius   *1960*
Spanish Ballads   *1960*
The Poem of the Cid   *1959*

W. S. MERWIN

SELECTED
TRANSLATIONS
1948-1968

ATHENEUM

New York

1968

A number of the poems in this book have been translated from French versions in *Trésor de la Poésie Universelle*, edited by Caillois and Lambert, published by Éditions Gallimard, Paris, 1958; the translations appear on pages 3 (originally in P. Gilbert, *La Poésie Egyptienne*), 7, 8 (originally from L. Laloy, *Choix de poésies Chinoises*), 15 (originally from J. Amrouche, *Chants Berbères de la Kabylie*), 17 (originally from no. 928, Journal Asiatique, trans. by N. K. Dimitrien-O. Chatskaya), 19 (originally from J. Lassaigne and I. Voronca, *Chants de Mort*), 21 (originally from K. Rasmussen, *Du Groenland au Pacifique*), 28 (originally from J. C. de Abreu, *Légendes, croyances et talismans des Indiens de l'Amazonie*), 33, 34, 36, 37 (originally from J. Markale, *Les Grands Bards Gallois*).

The three Kabylian poems on page 14 are translated from *Poésie Populaire des Kabyles*, recueillies par Pierre Savignac, Paris, 1964.

The Five Songs of Dahomey on page 16 are translated from *Chants du Dahomey et du Niger*, recueillies et traduits par Paul Mercier, Paris, 1950.

Page 22, translated from *Poèmes Eskimos*, by Paul Emil Victor, Paris, 1958.

Pages 23, 24, 25, 26 and 27, translated from *Literatura Inca*, Selección Basadre, Biblioteca de Cultura Peruana, Paris, 1938.

Page 24, translated from *Canciones de los Indios Pampas*, by Hernan Deibe, Buenos Aires, 1946.

Pages 39 and 41, translated from *Chants Populaires des Grecs*, translated by Matsie Hadjilazaros, Paris, 1951.

Pages 44 and 45, translated from *Anthologie des Chansons Populaires Grecques*, Paris, 1967.

The Catullus translation on page 50 was originally published in W. S. Merwin's *The Drunk in the Furnace*, Macmillan, New York, 1960.

The Sixth Satire of Persius is from *The Satires of Persius*, translated by W. S. Merwin, Indiana University Press, Bloomington, 1961.

The translations of anonymous Spanish poems on pages 61–71 were originally published in *Spanish Ballads*, translated by W. S. Merwin, Doubleday Anchor, New York, 1961.

The translations of poems by Lorca on pages 82, 83, 84 and 85 were originally published by New Directions in *The Selected Poems of Federico García Lorca*, copyright 1955 by New Directions Publishing Corporation.

The translations of poems by Borges on pages 86 and 87 are from *Jorge Luis Borges Selected Poems 1923–1968*, edited by Norman Thomas di Giovanni, published by Seymour Lawrence/Delacorte Press and copyright © 1968 by Editores Emecé, S.A., and Norman Thomas di Giovanni.

The translations of poems by Nicanor Parra on pages 101, 103, 106 and 109 are from *Poems and Anti-Poems* by Nicanor Parra, New Directions, 1968, copyright © 1967 by Nicanor Parra.

The translations of poems by Jean Follain on pages 135–141 are part of *Selected Poems of Jean Follain*, translated by W. S. Merwin, to appear in 1969 with the original French, which is copyright 1953, © 1960, 1964 by Éditions Gallimard.

The translations of Tyutchev, Blok, Esenin and Mandelstam were commissioned by Olga Carlisle and will appear in her critical anthology of Russian poetry, *Poets on Street Corners*, Random House, New York, 1969.

Some of these translations have appeared in the following publications: *Afrasian Magazine; An Anthology of French Poetry from Nerval to Valéry; An Introduction to African Literature; Burning Deck; Chelsea; Encounter; The Hudson Review; The Journal of Creative Behavior; Latitudes; The Nation; Poetry; The Sea and the Honeycomb; The Southern Review; The Times Literary Supplement;* a number of the translations were originally broadcast on the BBC Third Programme.

IN MEMORY OF

LAURENCE G. SAMPSON

WHO FIRST TAUGHT ME TO LOVE ANOTHER LANGUAGE

FOREWORD

A S THE TITLE INDICATES, these translations are taken from
the work of twenty years. The originals are native to
widely scattered periods and poetic conventions. I can speak only
subjectively of what the extremes share.

They were not all undertaken with the same ostensible pur-
pose. Some are testimony to old affections that have survived
such representation. Many are relics of the same kind of search
that prompts us, in our time, to read translations of poems: a
wish to embrace, even through wrappings, poetry that was
written from perspectives revealingly different from our own.
Some of them were commissioned.

I began translating with the idea that it could teach me
something about writing poetry. The great exemplar, of course,
was Pound. The neo-Flaubertian image of poetry as a "craft"
was in all the ikons I could see. Unfortunately something of the
"how" of writing poetry is probably always important, a re-
minder of the ambivalences of our imperfection and our artifice.
And every way of learning it, (and the learning itself as it is
acquired), has peculiar dangers. Translation may be no more
dangerous than any other to a growing recognition of the true
original that, in del Vasto's words, "tastes of the source." It is
love, I imagine, more than learning, that may eventually make
it possible to be aware of the living resonance before it has
words, to keep the distinction clear between mere habit and the
style that is some part, at least, of the man, and will impel one
to be wary of any skill coming to shadow and doctor the source,
any deftness usurping the authority it was reared to serve.
"When I pronounce men to be quick of hearing," Chuang Tzu
wrote, "I do not mean that they hearken to anything else, but
that they hearken to themselves." Which of course, is the true

and exacting vocation of the poet's ear, a matter of origin before it is one of learning. But every time the words are found, the finding is a contribution to learning as well, and it may be in the interest of clarity if some of the learning is obviously distinct from the particular source in oneself.

When I was still at college I made the pilgrimage to St. Elizabeth's to see Pound. He spoke of the value of translation as a means of continually sharpening a writer's awareness of the possibilities of his own language. He meant English, not any personal idiom of mine (I knew perfectly well that I had none at the time) and I still approach translation as a relatively anonymous activity in which whatever in the result may appear to be mine comes there simply because that is how the language, in the always elaborate given circumstances, sounds most alive to me. Pound also urged—at that point and to me, at least—the greatest possible fidelity to the original, including its sounds.

And I have not come to use translation as a way of touching off writing that then became deliberately, specially, or ostentatiously my own. On the contrary, I have felt impelled to keep translation and my own writing more and more sharply separate. This has been true not only when I knew enough of a language to be able to approach the original, up to a point, on my own, but also in those translations from languages which I do not know at all, in which I have had to rely on intermediary parsings and impressions, with the extra risks that that involves.

I must make clear what part of this collection falls into that second category. The only languages outside English in which I have any proficiency at all are romance languages, particularly French and Spanish. But I long ago forgot most of what Latin I ever learned, and more recently most of what Portuguese I ever knew; my reading Italian (which was all I had) was never anything but laborious and uncertain. So the Persius, for example, was composed with the help of every previous translation I could find, and whatever line-by-line notes I could lay hands on, and was then gone over by a scholar; I could certainly not have managed it with nothing but the text and a dictionary.

And as for the other languages—I know no Chinese, and the translations are from other versions. Where I could I used several other versions, and where possible I preferred to work from a previous translation in some language other than English, which would be less likely to afford suggestions. I managed to do this with most of the poems from languages I don't know at all. The Welsh and Irish poems, for instance, in their present forms, are based on French rather than on English forbears. No one who wants to read those poems for the purposes of scholarship is likely to be interested in my versions anyway, but I have not wilfully gone farther from what I thought was the original sense than the translations from which I was working had done. The same is true of the Greek poems, though there I occasionally condensed in the interests of a sharpness that I did not think was a disservice to the original. The poems from the more exotic, and from the "primitive" languages were all taken from French or Spanish translations, except the Vietnamese poems, which were done in collaboration with Nguyen Ngoc Bich, who supplied the literal English. I have forgotten almost all of the little German I once knew, and the versions of German poems were made with the help of bi-lingual editions and a dictionary, except for the Bobrowski poem, which was translated in collaboration with Jean-Pierre Hammer. The Tyutchev, Blok, Esenin and Mandelstam poems were translated in collaboration with Olga Carlisle, and the Brodsky poems in collaboration with Wladimir Weidlé.

W. S. M.

CONTENTS

Contents

xiii

Contents

W. S. MERWIN

SELECTED TRANSLATIONS
1948-1968

Death is before me today
like health to the sick
like leaving the bedroom after sickness.

Death is before me today
like the odor of myrrh
like sitting under a cloth on a day of wind.

Death is before me today
like the odor of lotus
like sitting down on the shore of drunkenness.

Death is before me today
like the end of the rain
like a man's home-coming after the wars abroad.

Death is before me today
like the sky when it clears
like a man's wish to see home after numberless years of captivity.

1960   (Indicates date of translation)

Oh the sound of her silk sleeves
no longer
oh the dust deepening
in the jade courtyard
the vacant room cold
abandoned
the doors
double-barred and their bars
littered with fallen leaves
oh if anyone looks now
for the beauty
of that woman where can it be found
I feel my heart
to which rest will not come

1967

I wake and my bed is gleaming with moonlight

Frozen into the dazzling whiteness I look up
To the moon herself
And lie thinking of home

1966

Where the mist has torn
The hills are the colors of spring
The sky is whitening
Not many stars are left
The fragment of moon is going out
But your face in the early light
Glitters
Now we must separate

After all the words
Nothing is eased
Turn your head I have something to add
You will remember
My skirt of green silk woven loosely
The new grass will remind you of it everywhere

1966

AUTUMN NIGHT

Tu Fu   Chinese   8th century

The dew falls, the sky is a long way up, the brimming waters
    are quiet.
On the empty mountain in the companionless night doubtless
    the wandering spirits are stirring.
Alone in the distance the ship's lantern lights up one motionless
    sail.
The new moon is moored to the sky, the sound of the beetles
    comes to an end.
The chrysanthemums have flowered, men are lulling their
    sorrows to sleep.
Step by step along the verandah, propped on my stick, I keep
    my eyes on the Great Bear.
In the distance the celestial river leads to the town.

1962

THE LAKE OF THE TEN
THOUSAND MOUNTAINS

Mong Hao-Jan   Chinese   8th century

I throw the line in from this little island.
The water is clear and my heart is protected.
The fish pass under the trees of the lake.
Along the promontory monkeys swing on the vines.
The wandering beauty of former days took off her necklace
in these mountains, the legend says.
I look for her but I have not found her.
The songs of the rowers lose the way to the moon.

1962

THE IDEAL RETREAT

Khong Lo   Vietnamese   medieval   Ly Dynasty

I will choose a place where the snakes feel safe.
All day I will love that remote country.
At times I will climb the peak of its lonely mountain
to stay and whistle until the sky grows cold.

1967   translated with NGUYEN NGOC BICH

9

AUTUMN

Ngo Chi Lan   Vietnamese   15th century

Sky full of autumn
earth like crystal
news arrives from a long way off following one wild goose.
The fragrance gone from the ten foot lotus
by the Heavenly Well.
Beech leaves
fall through the night onto the cold river,
fireflies drift by the bamboo fence.
Summer clothes are too thin.
Suddenly the distant flute stops
and I stand a long time waiting.
Where is Paradise
so that I can mount the phoenix and fly there?

1968   translated with NGUYEN NGOC BICH

WINTER

Ngo Chi Lan   Vietnamese   15th century

Lighted brazier
small silver pot
cup of Lofu wine to break the cold of the morning.
The snow
makes it feel colder inside the flimsy screens.
Wind lays morsels of frost on the icy pond.
Inside the curtains
inside her thoughts
a beautiful woman.
The cracks of doors and windows
all pasted over.
One shadowy wish to restore the spring world:
a plum blossom already open on the hill.

1968   translated with NGUYEN NGOC BICH

A WOODCUTTER ON HIS WAY
HOME

Anonymous   Vietnamese   18th century

Here and there little breezes stir the rushes.
At dusk the birds hurry as though they were lost.
Loaded with wood he moves slowly homeward.
He moves slowly, knowing the way.

1967   translated with NGUYEN NGOC BICH

THE SUBSTITUTED POEM
OF LAUREATE QUYNH

Anonymous   Vietnamese   folk poem

This is what the professor wrote home, listen:
tell my wife not to get heated up.
I have got it all the way north here perfectly limp.
Down south there she had better look to her clam.
Is it still tight and winding like a gopher's burrow
or is it gaping by now like a catfish grotto?
Tell her to hang onto it even if it gives her a fight.
I will be home in a couple of days.

1967   translated with NGUYEN NGOC BICH

I want someone to go out to the plain
work till evening
come back with the others
look in at the window to see what she is doing
fall between her thighs
and she will wake even if she is not sleeping.

———

God of this year, I implore you,
you that are angry with me
as though I had killed your father,
you gave flour to everybody
except me. To me you left
bran, saying, Take that or nothing.
I beg you by Saint Moulani, pity me
oh my God,
angry as though I had smashed up a holy place.

———

Oh sun rising
who light everything
in the name of God please
show me how to get to you
so I can arrive some day
now the suffering has stopped
or else it will start again.

1967

BERBER SONG

Kabylia   Anonymous folk song

She has fallen in the dance,
None of you knows her name.
A silver amulet
Moves between her breasts.

She has hurled herself into the dance.
Rings chime on her ankles.
Silver bracelets.

For her I sold
An apple orchard.

She has fallen in the dance.
Her hair has come loose.

For her I sold
My field of olive trees.

She has hurled herself into the dance.
Her collar of pearls glittered.

For her I sold
My orchard of fig trees.

She has hurled herself into the dance.
A smile flowered on her.

For her I sold
All my orange trees.

1962

15

FIVE SONGS OF DAHOMEY

Anonymous

The time will come even yet when we will dance there
And we will say look there are the girls we will marry
And the sky will clear.

———

We were dispersed one by one and the dry season came.
And we will come back again and we will meet.
The man who has no field, when he dances nobody knows it.

———

Night is turning into day
And the clouds are being swept across the sky.
Those who will buy you are twisting the ropes for you.

———

Early in the morning I say good-bye to those who have cut
    down the big tree and I put on my gear and I say
    that I am setting out on a journey.

Death is in this country from his hole to his head and you
    put on your gear and you say that you are setting
    out on a journey?

———

Tomorrow I will be lying on the terrace
And they find me dead and the sun goes down
And goes in, red, shining,
And the hyena is restless but he will turn back.

1961

TATAR SONGS

Anonymous

I

The sun rises going the rounds
as though it were tied to the apple tree.
One day if we live we will be back
making the rounds like the sun.

II

Little finger painted with henna, little copper finger-nail, dice
    of gold,
is it possible to leave a lover in this world?

Because of the orchard the sun does not pass my window.
As for me I have turned yellow, shrivelled by love.

Do not whiten the roof tree of the low house.
I am alone, I am unhappy, do not be cruel to me.

Why do you look out the door all the time?
I would give my life for the darkness of your eyes.

The child of the *bai* drinks water from a golden cup.
Under the moon a cloud, the moon's child.
And I, I have turned yellow, withered by love.

III

My beloved, the face is covered with blood.
The falcon's face, covered with blood.
The wind blew, a curl of hair came loose.
A wick took it, and the face covered with blood.

I built a house and it was a mirage.
But it was a shelter for my whole life.
The point of my stick was not solid
and our night had its danger.

I am dying because I always watched the road.
I looked to right and to left.
Neither your nor I will ever be done
watching the road, watching the road.

The seas turn into horses
and cupbearers.
I drank to quiet my sorrow
but it grew wilder all the time.

1962

SONG FOR THE DEAD

Roumanian   Anonymous folk poem

The evening becomes evening.
No one will shelter you.
And at that time
The otter will come toward you
To make you afraid.
But do not be afraid.
Receive her as your sister.
The otter knows
The order of the rivers,
The lay of the fords,
Will get you across,
Will save you from drowning,
Will carry you
To the cold sources
To refresh you
After the shudder of death.

Also before you
The wolf will appear
To make you afraid
But do not be afraid.
Receive him as your brother.
The wolf knows
The order of the forests,
The grain of the paths,
He will lead you
On the level road
To a king's son,
To paradise
Where life is good,

The hill for playing:
There is your place;
The field of peonies:
There is your heart.

1960

Into my head rose
the nothings
my life day after day
but I am leaving the shore
in my skin boat
It came to me that I was in danger
and now the small troubles
look big
and the ache
that comes from the things
I have to do every day
big

But only one thing
is great
only one
This
In the hut by the path
to see the day
coming out of its mother
and the light filling the world

1967

Anonymous   Eskimo

The dead who climb up to the sky
climb up steps
to the sky
up worn steps
all the dead who climb up to the sky
on worn steps
worn from the other side
worn from the inside
climb up to the sky

1967

ICHI THE DWARF

Anonymous   Quechuan   Peru

In Qjelle Huanca the earth opened and a dwarf popped out. He was naked and his hair was bright red like a fire. He sat down on a stone, and for the fun of it he brandished his lighted hair. His little lively eyes, like small coals, stared at the landscape in wonder, and because it was cold he began to cry like a sucking pig.

Then that little dwarf began to leap around among the rocks and crags and his scarlet hair caught in the thick leaves and fig branches and tangled him. At midnight he beat his belly like a drum and the raw sound rebounded from hill to hill. In the quiet afternoons he blew on his pipe and the flute warbled and trilled, but what he liked best of all was to frighten the men working in the fields. Whenever he found them gathering wood he would growl, he would give a low growl.

He sang, too, under the ground, and his songs went up into the air in the same way that the water of the marshes turns into clouds. When dawn rose into the heavens the far away songs of the little dwarf Ichi woke the children, and the calves lowed sweetly.

1959

THE RAINBOW

Anonymous   Quechuan   Peru

There was a fine rain at daybreak. The whole sky began to shine. The rainbow was born out of a marsh and he bent like a great bow from Pocyaccho to Pitacchopis.

He is afraid of the stares of men, which are too quick and piercing for him, and he retreats into the sky like a string of colors.

Some boys went to look for his feet. His toes are made of crystal, so he can hide them, and the boys could not find them. Then the boys threw stones at the rainbow.

When he enters the body of a man or a woman they become very sick and to cure them they are given a ball of seven-colored wool to unwind.

1959

ARAWI

Anonymous   Quechuan   Peru

I have lost my dove.
Wandering, I call to her in a loud voice.
Everyone who finds me says,
"Why did you love her?"
    Where have you flown?
Who have you left here to console me?
Like a dove whose wings have been cut off
I will die walking back and forth.
    Come back, dove whom I cherished.
How long must I wait for you?
In the nest, where we should be,
Now the birds of night raise their moans.

1959

BEAN FLOWER

Anonymous   Quechuan   Peru

Bean flower,
Black and white,
Like the heart of that man
Who loves two women.

Long live the apple.
Its tears are sweet.
This world has reason
To be bitter.

Little star of heaven
Lend me your brightness,
For the life of this world
Is a dark night.

1959

MY SPOUSE CHUNAYCHUNAY

Anonymous   Quechuan   Peru

My spouse, Chunaychunay,
Sweetly you carry me.

And what you say to me is sweet.
You, Wichiri,
Your cruel father
Stole from my mother
Her horses and saddled mules.

You wander by the river
With a blazing club
Abusing me because I am an orphan.
In the midst of many
Rags I sleep.
I live among miseries.

For your sake I will go.
Thus I sleep, I sleep.
Your net catches two abreast,
Rain, giver of water.

Oh Chunaychunay, brotherly heart,
Portion of the great feast
Which now will never return.
Do nothing to me, Putti,
For today my heart was brought to tears.

1959

THE CREATION OF THE MOON

Anonymous   Caxinua   Amazon

The man cut his throat and left his head there.
The others went to get it.
When they got there they put the head in a sack.
Farther on the head fell out onto the ground.
They put the head back in the sack.
Farther on the head fell out again.
Around the first sack they put a second one that was thicker.
But the head fell out just the same.
It should be explained that they were taking the head to show to
    the others.
They did not put the head back in the sack.
They left it in the middle of the road.
They went away.

They crossed the river.
But the head followed them.
They climbed up a tree full of fruit
to see whether it would go past.

The head stopped at the foot of the tree
and asked them for some fruit.
So the men shook the tree.
The head went to get the fruit.
Then it asked for some more.

So the men shook the tree
so that the fruit fell into the water.
The head said it couldn't get the fruit from there.
So the men threw the fruit a long way
to make the head go a long way to get it so they could go.

While the head was getting the fruit
the men got down from the tree and went on.

The head came back and looked at the tree
and didn't see anybody
so went on rolling down the road.

The men had stopped to wait
to see whether the head would follow them.
They saw the head come rolling.

They ran.
They got to their hut they told the others that the head
was rolling after them and to shut the door.

All the huts were closed tight.
When it got there the head commanded them to open the doors.
The owners would not open them because they were afraid.

So the head started to think what it would turn into.
If it turned into water they would drink it.
If it turned into earth they would walk on it.
If it turned into a house they would live in it.
If it turned into a steer they would kill it and eat it.
If it turned into a cow they would milk it.
If it turned into wheat they would eat it.
If it turned into a bean they would cook it.
If it turned into the sun
When men were cold it would heat them.
If it turned into rain the grass would grow and the animals
        would crop it.

So it thought, and it said, "I will turn into the moon."
It called, "Open the doors, I want to get my things."
They would not open them.

The head cried. It called out, "At least give me
my two balls of twine."
They threw out the two balls of twine through a hole.
It took them and threw them into the sky.

It asked them to throw it a little stick too
to roll the thread around so it could climb up.

Then it said, "I can climb, I am going to the sky."
It started to climb.

The men opened the doors right away.
The head went on climbing.
The men shouted, "You going to the sky, head?"
It didn't answer.

As soon as it got to the Sun
it turned into the Moon.
Toward evening the Moon was white, it was beautiful.
And the men were surprised
to see that the head had turned into the Moon.

1962

THREE PAMPAS INDIAN SONGS

Anonymous

If I have two horses
we will go one on each

If I have only one
I will take you behind me

I am very poor
but we will go

We will travel ten days.
The length of this country!

I don't say it will be tomorrow
that we will go

But we will go.

―――――

When I was a good and quick little girl
they treated me like a treasure

oh heart!

Many suns and many moons I saw
time passes

oh heart!

How I have changed. I am not a girl now
I am very old

oh heart!

What is the use of grieving
if nobody will listen

oh heart!

———

Necessity has made us all very poor.
The best families could not keep their riches.
If a poor man comes to a hut he sees the hearth cold.
And he hears, "I am poor. I do not even have fire any more."

We bury the dark thought in the ashes
And say nothing, not to add to our trouble.
They have taken everything from us: land, family,
Flocks, soul. Now we do not even have fire.

1958

YSCOLAN

Myrddyn   Welsh   circa 6th century

Your horse is black your cloak is black
your face is black you are black
you are all black—is it you Yscolan?

I am Yscolan the seer
my thoughts fly they are covered with clouds.
Is there no reparation then for offending the Master?

I burned a church I killed the cows that belonged to a school
I threw the Book into the waves
my penance is heavy.

Creator of living things you
greatest of all my protectors forgive me.
He that betrayed you deceived me.

I was fastened for a whole year
at Bangor under the piles of the dam.
Try to think what I suffered from the sea worms.

If I had known what I know now
the liberty of the wind in the moving tree tops
that crime could not be laid to me.

1962

THE GLORY OF TALIESIN

Welsh   circa 6th century

Messengers came to me they crowded up to me
to tell my heart of the war tomorrow.

The drink of Beli is like the foam the oar lifts at sea.

Like a bright shield is the back of a shadow
like anger and indignation
out of a city where nine hundred governors are dead.

There will be a battle at Menao fierce vengeance
and on Conwy cliff a fight without mercy

cold death will be the lot of the Muse
it is natural to love her.

To the violence of the blows of Edern's sword
three men will fall who could not be dissuaded

three fleets on the great current
will foretell the day of darkness
and three nights of battle across
three noble countries.

The ships will be coffins

three from each of the three
three sins
and the mountain of Eryry will be the hill of darkness.

There will be one army of Saxons a second a third.

In the country of Kymrys widowhood
is waiting for the wives.

At Kynon's arrival look for the fire to break out.
Kadwaladyr will mourn for him
he will visit his own torment on the countryside
burning the straw and the roofs.

After that a marvellous thing.
From a man and his brother's daughter
steel will be born
the line of Anarawd.
From him will descend the Red
the wise the cunning
who will neither spare nor defend
brother nor cousin.

At the sound of the warrior's horn
nine hundred will lose hope
as disaster arrives everywhere.

You will see your glory grow leaves
however your heart may have been oppressed.

1962

DEATH SONG OF KYNDYLAN

Welsh   circa 7th century

White village in the woods
its grass covered with blood
all the time ever since it was built.

White village ever since it was built
blood lay on the green around it
under the feet of its warriors.

White village in the valley
would have celebrated a battle won.
Have the people who lived there come home?

White village between Tren and Throdwyth
saw shields broken
instead of oxen resting.

White village between Tren and Travel
saw blood on its grass
instead of its fallow under the plow.

1962

THE SONG OF CELLACH

Anonymous   Irish   12th century

I greet the white morning
stepping on the earth like a flame,
I greet its sender,
the new morning, the conqueror.

White morning in your pride,
brother of the bright sun,
I greet you, white morning,
lighting my book.

My marked book tells me
my life hangs in the balance,
I am afraid of Malcroin,
he that will strike me.

Hooded crow, hooded crow,
gray cloak, sharp beak,
I know what you want,
you're no friend of Cellach.

Croaking raven,
bird, if you're hungry,
wait in the castle;
you'll dine on my body.

The kite from the cliff of Cluain Eo
will come hungry to the brawl,
he'll hook me in blue talons,
he'll hang on.

The fox in the dark wood
will be with them, he wastes no time,
he'll eat my blood and flesh
in cold crevices with one entrance.

The wolf in the castle
that's east of Druin meic Dair
in one hour will be standing over me,
head of the pack.

I had a dream,
it was Wednesday night:
the wild dogs dragged me
east, west, through the red ferns.

I had a dream
they took me into a valley,
four of them held me,
I think they did not bring me back.

I had a dream
my followers took me to their house
and poured out a drink for me
and drank to my health.

Oh little wren with hardly a tail,
shame, shame: did you sell your song?
Coming to warn that I'm here,
and ending my life.

1962

SONG OF EXILE

Anonymous   Greek   modern ballad collection

Already the month
of May and the spring,
almost summer;
branches swell, flowers
open; now he who is not
in his own place
longs to go to his country,
saddles his horse at night,
spends the dark hours
over the horse shoes, makes
silver shoes for his horse,
nailed with gold nails, puts on
spurs, sword on his belt; the girl
who loves him
is holding a candle
so he can see, in one hand
the candle, in the other
the wineglass; each time
she fills it again for him
she says again, "Master,
take me, take me with you, take me
where you go, I
will cook so you can eat,
make the bed so you can sleep,
be earth so you can walk on me,
a bridge so you can cross over,
a goblet of silver
for you to drink wine from,
for you to drink your
wine from, and see

my reflection in."
"Where I am going, little one,
is beyond women.
Wolves hold the mountains
and thieves the passes
to lay hands on you, girl,
and make me a slave."

1960

MAIDO

Anonymous   Greek   modern ballad collection

Maido is there, Maido
in a palace of mirrors
holding a mirror
up to her beauty,
oh beauty
standing like a cypress;
all of one evening she wanted
Costas in bed with her.
"Here I am, Maido, I've come.
I'm not afraid of John.
John's off on the mountain,
he's gone hunting stags,
I hope to God it rains and snows
and the Danube overflows
and carries all the bridges away
and John on the mountain.
I hope to God the bears eat him."
And they are still there talking
and here is John, come home
with a load of stags, with a train
of live stags and tame bears,
with the reins of his horse hauling trees
torn up by the roots.
He spurs his horse to the door
"Maido, come down, get the meat."
"John, I'm afraid of the stags,
and I'm more afraid of the bears.
Take them to your mother.
They don't frighten her."
So he rides to his mother's. "Mother,

come down, Mother, open the door,
and get the meat. Maido
is afraid of the stags,
and she's more afraid of the bears."
"She's not afraid of the stags,
it's not the bears she's afraid of.
She's afraid because she's deceived you,
and Costas is there with her."
With one foot he smashes the door
and she falls limp in a corner.
"Costas, you devil's baby,
what's your excuse?"
"It's your Maido; she called to me
from the window."
He takes out his little knife
and cuts off her head.
On a silver plate he carries it
to his mother-in-law.
"Mother-in-law, come down
and see what I've brought you."
She laughs as she goes to uncover it,
then she covers it, weeping.
"Oh, what have you done,
dog, murderer, head
for curses to ride on!
And what are courtrooms for?
You could have taken her there.
And what are judges for?
They could have judged her."
He puts the head in a little bag,
takes it to the miller.
"Good mill, grind, grind
Maido's head to coal dust,
to coal dust to make
black bread,
to coal dust

to make ink
so that those who can write
can write the head of Maido."

1960

FOUR GREEK POEMS

Anonymous

Liberty

Down there
on the shore
down there
on a beach
there is an eagle lying
weighted with snow
and he calls on the sun
to shine: Shine my old sun
shine
my golden eye
so the snow will
melt and my wings
be free
and I will fly
like the other birds
and write a message
and send it to the desert
to my palaces
my high
dwellings

Exile

In a foreign country
wear black
the heart does

The Crypts

Here
in this church
put away
the girls sleep
lemon trees
the boys sleep
cypruses
the old men sleep
torn up by the roots
the women sleep
splintered doors
the children sleep
dried apples

Swallow

A swallow
from the white sea
starts saying: March March
February
old friend old fright
snow snow
rain rain
never mind
you too smell the spring

1967

Salutations, girl with nose none of the smallest
Nor exquisite foot nor eyes quite like jet
Nor delicate fingers nor mouth any too clean
Nor a tongue notable for its elegance,
Mistress of that dissipated Formian.
You pass for a beauty in the provinces?
They compare you with my Lesbia?
Oh foolish and unlicked generation !

1958

Let us live, my Lesbia, and let us love;
As for the buzzings of censorious
Old men, let them be all one for us.
Suns can endure their settings and return
But for us once our short light is gone
Night is a sleep from which we never wake.
Give me a thousand kisses, then a hundred,
Another thousand and another
Hundred, and another, and more thousands
Till we have lost all count, so that those
Who'd fix us with their evil eyes
Can't turn the count of our kisses against us.

1958

Like a god he seems to me who beholds you,
Even greater than the gods, if that could be,
Who sits facing you, and everlastingly
    Gazes, and hears

Your sweet laughter which in my wretchedness
Uproots all my senses; Lesbia, you no more
Than appear before me, and at once I have
    No voice in my mouth,

My tongue is benumbed too, and a thin flame
Slips through my limbs, my ears begin ringing
With a din of their own, and twofold night
    Falls on my eyes.

Catullus, idleness is your undoing.
From idleness you grow overwrought, you flare up
Too much. Kings have been lost, and rich cities,
    Through idleness.

1958

Caelius, my Lesbia, Lesbia, that same
Same Lesbia, whom alone Catullus,
More than himself and all that he owned, loved,
Now at street corners and in alleys milks
The scions of high-minded Remus.

1958

Furius and Aurelius, bound to Catullus
Though he penetrate to the ends of the Indies
Where the eastern ocean crashing in echoes
  Pours up the shore,

Or into Hyrcania, soft Arabia,
Among Tartars or the archers of Parthia,
Or where the Nile current, seven times the same,
  Colors the waters,

Or through the beetling Alps, by steep passes, should come
To look on the monuments of great Caesar,
Gaul, the Rhine, and at the world's bitter end
  The gruesome Britons,

Friends, both prepared to share with me all these
Or what else the will of heaven may send,
To my mistress take these few sentiments,
  Put none too nicely:

Let her spread for her lechers and get her pleasure,
Lying wide to three hundred in one heat,
Loving none truly but leaving them every one
  Wrung out and dropping;

But as for my love, let her not count on it
As once she could: by her own fault it died
As a flower at the edge of a field, which the plow
  Roots out in passing.

1958

THE SIXTH SATIRE

Persius   Latin   34–62 A.D.

Has the season, descending into winter,
Fetched you, by now, Bassus, to your Sabine fireside?
Is your strung harp alive to the chastening plectrum,
Oh artisan without peer at ordering in verse
The primal elements of our language and waking
The virile tones of the Latin lyre, oh marvellous
Old man, alive with the merriment of youth and with
Songs, besides, which are gay without being dirty.
For the moment the Ligurian coast and my own
Winter sea offer me their little warmth; from a breach
In the bastion of towering cliffs at the sea's edge
A deep valley here runs inland. As Ennius put it:
"Citizens, you would do well to know the harbor
Of Luna"—speaking in his right mind, when he had
Done dreaming that he was Homer, the Lydian,
Descendant of Pythagoras's peacock.

      Here I live, neither troubled by the multitude
Nor flustered by the south wind's ill humors menacing
My flocks, nor miserable because that corner
Of my neighbor's fields is richer than my own. Even
Though men whose birth was beneath mine were to grow rich,
Every one of them, I would still not get all hunched up
And scrawny with fussing over it, nor go without
Sauce for my meat, nor descend to sniffing the seals
Of wine jars to see whether the rank stuff could possibly
Still be swallowed. People aren't all alike. You get twins, with
The same horoscope, turning out to have different
Temperaments. One man has a habit (but only
On birthdays) of sprinkling his dry greens with brine
Which the sly fellow buys by the cupful—and you can tell

By the way he dribbles the pepper onto the platter
That the stuff is holy. Here's another, a large-mannered
Young man who will shortly have eaten his way through
A huge inheritance. As for me, I try
To make the most of things, without being so lavish
As to feed my freedmen on turbot, nor of so
Sophisticated a palate that I can tell
Hen thrush from cock thrush by the taste.

      Live on your own harvest, mill your own grain, that's as it
Should be. Why should you worry? You have only
To harrow again to have another crop on the way.
But obligations nag at your elbow: there's that
Friend who washed up on the Bruttian rocks, in the wreckage
Of his ship, and hauled himself in. He's penniless.
His possessions, accompanied by his useless prayers,
Have settled under the Ionian Sea, and he himself
Is stretched on the beach with the great statues of the gods
From off the vessel's stern strewn round him, while already
The gulls are gathering on the splintered ship's timbers.
Why not divest yourself of a plot of good farmland
And give it to the unfortunate man, and save him
From toting his picture around on a blue board?
Are you hesitant because your heir would be angry
At a cut like that in the property, and after holding
A cheap funeral supper over you, would stuff your bones
Unperfumed into the urn, never bothering
To make sure that the cinnamon was fresh and the cassia
Unmixed with cherry, merely mumbling, "Thought you could
Shave bits off your estate and get away with it,
Did you?" And Bestius will drone on, libelling
The sages of Greece: "That's how it goes, ever since
That neutered brand of philosophy was imported
Into this city with the dates and pepper, our
Farmhands have been getting dainty. Now they've taken
To polluting their gruel with rich oil." But why
Should you worry about this sort of thing once you're on

The other side of the fire? As for you, my heir,
Whoever you are, leave the crowd for a minute and lend me
Your attention.

       Haven't you heard, friend? A laurelled
Dispatch has arrived from Caesar, announcing
Victory, the pick of the Germans routed—and already
They're sweeping the dead ashes from the altars, and
Caligula's wife is seeing to the arrangements:
Bouquets of arms for over the gates, costumes for kings,
Yellow wigs for prisoners, and chariots, and monstrous
Models of the Rhine. I'm putting on a little show
Myself, to celebrate the occasion and the gods
And the Emperor's guiding spirit—with a hundred pairs
Of gladiators. Well who says I shouldn't? Who
Would dare to say I shouldn't. God help you if you don't
String along! Oh, and I'm having a largesse of bread,
And meat, and oil distributed to the populace.
Any objections? Speak up. "Oh no," you say, "Not with that
Field full of stones within easy range." Because even
If none of my father's sisters are left, and
I survive all my cousins, and my father's brother
Leaves no great-granddaughters, and my mother's sister
Dies without issue, and my grandmother is survived
By no other descendant, I can always take myself
Over to Bovillae, to the hill of Virbius
Where there's a wonderful selection of beggars, and there
I'll find me an heir in no time. Manius, for example—
"A son of the soil?" Well ask me who my own grandfather's
Grandfather was. Maybe I can tell you, though again
It might take a moment. But carry it back one more
Generation, then another, and sooner or later
You'll end up with a son of the soil. So if you're going to be
Clannish and stuffy about it, this Manius is really
A sort of great uncle indefinitely removed.
Besides, you've got a nerve, when you're ahead of me, grabbing
For my torch before I've finished my race. Think of me

As your private Mercury, for I come to you like
That god (in the pictures) with a moneybag in my hand.
Don't you want it? Are you determined not to be happy
With what I leave you? "It's not all here." All right, I spent
Some of it for my own uses, but whatever's left
Is all yours. Only you'll get nowhere if you expect me
To give an account of every cent I inherited
Ages ago, from Tadius. And don't come plying me
With fatherly maxims about investing capital
And living on the interest. "But what will be left?"
Left? Here, boy, don't lose a minute: pour out the oil.
Pour, I said! I want my cabbage drowned in it. Maybe
You think I'm going to confine myself on holidays
To smoked cheek of pork and split pig's ear garnished with
    nettles
So that on some future occasion a prodigal unripe
Sot, my heir, his guts stuffed with goose livers, and the fretful
Vein in his privates setting up a restive throbbing,
May piss into a high-born pussy. Or that I should
Abstain till I'm diaphanous so that his paunch
Can jiggle like a priest's.
        Go, peddle your soul
For lucre, and haggle, and drag the ends of the earth for
Merchandise. See to it that no one outdoes you
At slapping the fat of Cappadocian slaves, up on the
Auction block. Turn every penny into two. "I have. And
Into three. And four. I've got it up to ten." Well, make
A mark where you want me to stop and I'll inform Chrysippus
That you're the man to finish his unfinishable pile.

1959

Clothe him, in garments
They clothe him, with great sorrow,
For today he departs
From his house and where he was born.

Clothe him, in garments
They clothe him, with many laments,
For the blow struck in rage
Found no cure nor balm.

Clothe him, in garments
They clothe him, with many sighs,
The young men depart,
There is none who will bring up his sons.

Clothe him, in garments
They clothe him, with much grief,
The young men depart
And leave his house empty.

1957

Do not throw earth
On his lovely face,
For today he departs
From his house and his people.

Do not throw earth
on his colored eyes;
The young men go away,
None will bring up his darlings.

1957

LAMENT

Anonymous   Spanish   Medieval

On a dark night
My mother bore me.
They wrapped me in mourning.
Good luck I had none.

When I was born
The hour was waning,
No dog was heard,
No cock crowing.
No cock crowing,
No dog was heard,
Only my fortune
Cursing me.

Go, leave me,
You that are lucky;
Lay eyes on me
And ill luck will dog you.
When I was born
Omens foretold:
"If he loves women
He will eat scorn."

A sign of night
I was sired under:
Saturn reigning
In waning orbit.
My milk and cradle
Are the hard ground,
A bitch bore me,
No woman, no woman.

My mother, dying,
With sorrowing voice
By name named me
A luckless son.
Love, in a fury,
With his leigemen,
His bow in his hands,
Stands in my way.

Too great my love
Of your beauty,
Too great my sorrow;
Good luck I had none.

1957

MEDIEVAL LYRICS

Anonymous   Spanish

In Avila, my eyes,
In the town of Avila.

In Avila by the river
They killed my lover,
In the town of Avila.

———

I see they all lament.
I shall die silent.

———

My mother
Sent me to draw water,
Alone, and at such an hour.

———

The bee-keeper kissed me.
By the taste of honey I knew it was he.

———

Do not go out at night to go hunting, sir.
Because the night is dark, fair love.
And I die of fear.

———

Fine rain falling
And the night dark
And the shepherd a green boy.
I will not be safe.

She has lovely eyes
Which she never raises.

———

At the wedding
Everyone is singing
And the bride weeping.

1958

FIFTH *ROMANCE*
OF THE SEVEN PRINCES OF LARA

Anonymous   Spanish   late medieval

In sorrow I abide in Burgos,
Blind with weeping at my misfortunes,
Not knowing when the day rises
Nor when the night has come,
Were it not that with hard heart
Doña Lambra, who hates me,
Each day as dawn breaks
Sends to wake my grief also:
So that I may weep for my sons
One by one, every day
She has her men throw
Seven stones at my window.

1957

MELISELDA

Anonymous   Spanish   late medieval

If you know the pains of love,
In your grace, in your goodness,
Knight, if to France you go,
Ask for Gaiferos,
And tell him that his lady
Commends herself to him,
That his jousts and his journeys
Are famous among us,
And his courtliness
At praising the ladies.
Tell him for a certainty
That they will wed me:
Tomorrow I must marry
One from across the sea.

1958

THE ENCHANTED PRINCESS

Anonymous   Spanish   late medieval

The knight has gone hunting, hunting,
As often before,
His hounds are weary,
He has lost his falcon.
Against an oak he leaned,
It was marvellously high;
On a branch at the top
He saw a little princess;
The hair of her head
Covered all of that oak tree.
—Knight, do not be afraid,
Nor draw back with dread,
For I am the good King's daughter,
My mother is Queen of Castile.
Seven fairies bewitched me
In my nurse's arms
To stay for seven years
Alone on this mountain.
It is seven years today,
Or at dawn tomorrow.
Knight, in God's name I beg you,
Take me away with you,
To be your wife if you please,
Or if not, your mistress.—
—Wait for me, my lady,
Until dawn tomorrow.
I will go to my mother nearby
And ask her to advise me.—
The girl gave him an answer,
These are the words she spoke:

—Oh knight, you are wrong and foolish
To leave me here alone!—
But he goes to get advice
And leaves her on the mountain.
The advice that his mother gave him
Was to take her for his mistress.
When the knight returned to the place
He could not find the Princess.
He saw a great procession
Bearing her away.
The knight, when he beheld it,
Fell down onto the ground,
And when he came to his senses
His words were these:
—The knight who could lose such a thing
Deserves a heavy penance.
I will be my own judge,
I will pronounce my own sentence:
Let them cut off my feet and hands
And through the town drag me.

1957

THE PRISONER

Anonymous   Spanish   versions at different periods

It was May, the month of May,
When warm days are with us,
When the grain gets its growth
And the fields are in flower,
When the skylark sings
And the nightingale answers,
When those who are in love
Do love's bidding,
Except for me, living
In sorrow in this prison,
Not knowing when it is day
Nor when night has come
Except for a little bird
Which sang to me at dawn;
A man killed it with a crossbow,
God give him an ill reward!

1957

DON GARCÍA

Anonymous   Spanish   Renaissance

Don García is walking
Along the top of a wall,
With arrows of gold in one hand
And a bow in the other.
He calls down curses on Fortune,
He recounts her abuses:
When I was a child the King reared me,
God was a cloak around me;
A horse and arms he gave me
Excelling all others;
He gave me Doña María
To be my wife and consort,
He gave me a hundred maidens
To wait upon her,
He gave me the Castle of Uraña
As her dowry,
He gave me a hundred knights
To keep the castle,
He provided me with wine,
He provided me with bread,
He provided me with sweet water,
For there was none in the place.
The Moors laid siege to me there
On St. John's Day in the morning.
Seven years have come and gone
And the siege has not been lifted.
I have seen my people die
Because I had nothing to give them.
I set them up on the ramparts
With their weapons in their hands

So that the Moors should think
That they were ready for battle.
In the Castle of Uraña
There is only one loaf of bread.
If I give it to my children
What then of my wife?
If I were so base as to eat it
They would not forgive me.—
He broke the bread into four pieces
And flung it down into the camp.
One of the four pieces
Rolled to the King's feet:
—Allah, here is grief for my Moors!
Allah is pleased to afflict them.
From his castle's overabundance
He supplies our encampment!—
And he told them to sound the trumpets
And they lifted the siege.

1958

THE GRAY SHE-WOLF

Anonymous   Spanish   17th century?

As I was in my hut
Painting my shepherd's crook
The Pleiades were climbing
And the moon waning;
Sheep are poor prophets
Not to keep to the fold.
I saw seven wolves
Come up through a dark gully.
They cast lots as they came
To see who should enter the fold;
It fell to an old she-wolf,
Gray, grizzled and bow-legged,
With fangs lifting her lips
Like the points of knives.
Three times she circled the fold
And could take nothing;
Once more she went round it
And snatched the white lamb,
The Merino's daughter,
Niece of the earless ewe,
Which my masters were saving
For Easter Sunday.
—Come here, my seven pups,
Here, my bitch from Trujilla,
Here, you on the chain,
Run down the gray she-wolf.
If you fetch back the lamb
On milk and bread you will dine;
Fail to fetch her back,
You'll dine on my stick.—

On the heels of the she-wolf
They wore their nails down to crumbs;
Seven leagues they ran her
On the harsh mountains.
Climbing a little ravine,
The she-wolf begins to tire:
—Here, dogs, you can take the lamb,
As sound and well as ever.—
—We do not want the lamb
From your wolving mouth;
Your skin is what we want,
For a coat for the shepherd,
Your tail to make laces
To fasten his breeches,
Your head for a bag
To keep spoons in,
And your guts for lute strings
To make the ladies dance.

1957

THE CORPSE-KEEPER

Anonymous   Catalan   post-Renaissance

Seven years I have kept him, dead
And hidden in my chamber.
I change the shirt on him
Every holiday of the year.
I have anointed his face
With roses and white wine.
I have watched his bones laid bare
Of their white white flesh.
Alas, what can I do,
Wretch, in my disgrace?
Should I tell my father
He would say it is my lover;
Should I tell my mother
I would have no peace after;
Should I tell my sister
She knows nothing of love;
Should I tell my brother
He is the man to kill me;
Should I tell the constable
He would have me punished.
Better for me to say nothing,
To endure it and hold my tongue.
One day at my balcony,
Looking from my window,
I saw a huntsman passing
Who hunts in our crags.
—Huntsman, good huntsman,
One word, hear me:
Will you bury a dead body?
You will be rewarded.

And not in worthless coppers
But in gold and silver.—
Going down the stairs
Two thousand kisses I gave him:
—Farewell, delight of my life,
Farewell, delight of my soul;
It will not be long
Before I come and visit you.

1957

LAMENT FOR THE DEATH
OF GUILLÉN PERAZA

Anonymous   Spanish   Renaissance

Grieve, ladies, so may God keep you.
Guillén Peraza remained in Palma,
Withered, the flower of his face.

No palm are you, you are broom,
You are cypress of mournful bough,
You are misfortune, dire misfortune.

May molten stone buckle your fields,
May you see no pleasures, only sorrows,
May the sand-pits cover your flowers.

Guillén Peraza, Guillén Peraza,
Where is your shield, where is your spear?
By ill fortune all is ended.

1958

In Santiago the green
Jealousy seized me,
Night sits in the day,
I dream of vengeance.

Poplars of the thicket,
Where is my love?
If she were with another
Then I would die.

Clear Manzanares,
Oh little river,
Empty of water,
Run full of fire.

1950

Go, sighs,
Go there where you go always,
And if she is sleeping, my little one,
Forget her.

1950

SPANISH FOLK SONGS

Anonymous   19th century collection

Throw a crust to the dog
if you come to see me
because my mother sleeps as lightly
as a hare.

———

When they broke the news to me
that you've stopped loving me
even the house cat
looked at me and laughed.

———

You tell them everywhere
that I love you
and I loathe even the saint
you were named for.

———

I can't go to church
because I'm a cripple.
I'm going to the tavern
little by little.

———

We say good-bye to each other.
We say it again, sadly.
My heart hangs from the bars
of your balcony.

———

I am getting tired
of your love
because there aren't many chances
and you waste them.

————

If you don't come
to your window tonight
number me among the dead
in the morning.

————

I forsook father and mother
to go with you
and you left me alone
on the road.

————

Fancy hair-do
full of kiss-curls
and not even four chairs
in the house.

————

Little pearl, suit yourself when you marry:
your parents will die
and won't come from the other world
to see if you're happy.

————

God bless me, Father Adam,
how I love that woman!
The day I don't see her
I draw her picture on the wall.

————

Little beauty,
since I saw that calm face
the wings of my heart have fallen
over my feet.

———

Heart, I told you before,
and twice, and three times,
don't knock at that door.
No one will answer.

1957

I shall run through the shadow,
sleeping, sleeping, to see
if I can come where you are
who died, and I did not know.

Wait, wait; do not run;
wait for me in the dead water
by the lily that the moon
makes out of light; with the water
that flows from the infinite
into your white hand!
                        Wait;
I have one foot already through the black
mouth of the first nothing,
of the resplendent and blessed dream,
the bud of death flowering!

1949

I AM GOING
BECAUSE THE EAR OF WHEAT AND
THE DAWN ARE NOT MINE

León Felipe   Spanish   1884–

I have walked, lost, over the world, asking for bread and light.
And the sun is bread and light!
Look how he rises from the oven and ascends into the dawn for
    all,
with his double crown of flour and crystal! . . .
Oh ancient and generous God, banished by man!
You, always there, unfailing in the ear of wheat and in the dawn
and I here hungry and blind, with my beggar's cry lost again
    and again throughout history!

1960

THE DEAD

Pedro Salinas   Spanish   1892–1951

The first thing I forgot was your voice.
Now if you were to
speak here at my side
I would ask, "Who is that?"

After that I forgot your footstep.
If a shadow were to gutter
in the wind of flesh
I would not be sure it was you.

One by one all your leaves fell
before a winter: the smile,
the glance, the color of your clothes, the size
of your shoes.

Even then your leaves went on falling:
your flesh fell from you, your body.
I was left with your name, seven letters of you.
And you living,
desperately dying
in them, body and soul.
Your skeleton, its shape,
your voice, your laugh, seven letters, those letters.
And repeating them was your only life, your body.
I forgot your name.
The seven letters move about, unconnected,
unknown to each other.
They form advertisements in street-cars; letters
burn at night in colors,
they travel in envelopes shaping

other names.
There, everywhere, you go too,
all in pieces by now, dismantled, impossible.
There goes your name everywhere, which was you,
risen
toward various stupid heavens
in an abstract alphabetical glory.

1966

THE LITTLE MUTE BOY

Federico García Lorca   Spanish   1898–1936

The little boy was looking for his voice.
(The king of the crickets had it.)
In a drop of water
The little boy was looking for his voice.

I do not want it for speaking with;
I will make a ring of it
So that he can wear my silence
On his little finger.

In a drop of water
The little boy was looking for his voice.
(The captive voice, far away,
Put on a cricket's clothes.)

1954

HE DIED AT SUNRISE

Federico García Lorca   Spanish   1898–1936

Night of four moons
and only one tree,
only one shadow
and only one bird.

I track through my flesh
the trail of your lips.
The fountain kisses the wind
without touching it.

I bear the No that you gave me
in the palm of my hand,
like a wax lemon
almost white.

Night of four moons
and only one tree.
My love is spinning
on the point of a needle.

1954

CASIDA OF THE DARK DOVES

Federico García Lorca   Spanish   1898–1936

Through the branches of the laurel
I saw two dark doves.
The one was the sun,
The other the moon.
Little neighbors, I said to them,
Where is my tomb?
In my tail, said the sun.
In my throat, said the moon.
And I who was walking
With the earth at my belt
Saw two marble eagles
And a naked girl.
The one was the other
And the girl was no one.
Little eagles, I said to them,
Where is my tomb?
In my tail, said the sun.
In my throat, said the moon.
In the branches of the cherry tree
I saw two naked doves.
The one was the other
And both were no one.

1954

GACELA OF THE LOVE
THAT HIDES

Federico García Lorca   Spanish   1898–1936

*Only to hear
The bell of La Vela
I crowned you with a crown of verbena.*

Granada was a moon
Drowned among grasses.

*Only to hear
The bell of La Vela
I tore up my garden in Cartagena.*

Granada was a doe,
Pink, through the weathervanes.

*Only to hear
The bell of La Vela
I burned in your body
Not knowing whose it was.*

1954

PARTING

Jorge Luis Borges   Spanish   1899–

Three hundred nights like three hundred walls
must rise between my love and me
and the sea will be a black art between us.

Time with a hard hand will tear out
the streets tangled in my breast.
Nothing will be left but memories.
(O afternoons earned with suffering,
nights hoping for the sight of you,
dejected vacant lots, poor sky
shamed in the bottom of the puddles
like a fallen angel . . .
And your life that graces my desire
and that run-down and light-hearted neighborhood
shining today in the glow of my love . . .)

Final as a statue
your absence will sadden other fields.

1968

THE GENEROUS ENEMY

Jorge Luis Borges   Spanish   1899–

*In the year 1102, Magnus Barfod (the name means 'barefoot')
undertook the general conquest of the Irish kingdoms; it is said
that on the eve of his death he received this greeting from
Muirchertach, the King of Dublin:*

May gold and the storm fight on your side, Magnus Barfod.
May your fighting meet with good fortune, tomorrow, on the
    fields of my kingdom.
May your royal hands strike awe, weaving the sword's web.
May those who oppose your sword be food for the red swan.
May your many gods sate you with glory, may they sate you
    with blood.
May you be victorious in the dawn, King who tread upon
    Ireland.
May tomorrow shine the brightest of all your many days.
Because it will be your last. That I swear to you, King Magnus.
Because before its light is blotted out I will defeat you and blot
    you out, Magnus Barfod.

1968

WALKING AROUND

Pablo Neruda   Spanish   1904–

As it happens, I am tired of being a man.
As it happens I go into tailors' shops and movies
all shrivelled up, impenetrable, like a felt swan
navigating on a water of origin and ash.

The smell of barber shops makes me sob out loud.
I want nothing but the repose either of stones or of wool,
I want to see no more establishments, no more gardens,
nor merchandise, nor eyeglasses, nor elevators.

As it happens I am tired of my feet and my nails
and my hair and my shadow.
As it happens I am tired of being a man.

Just the same it would be delicious
to scare a notary with a cut lily
or knock a nun stone dead with one blow of an ear.
It would be beautiful
to go through the streets with a green knife
shouting until I died of cold.

I do not want to go on being a root in the dark,
hesitating, stretched out, shivering with dreams,
downwards, in the wet tripe of the earth,
soaking it up and thinking, eating every day.

I do not want to be the inheritor of so many misfortunes.
I do not want to continue as a root and as a tomb,
as a solitary tunnel, as a cellar full of corpses,
stiff with cold, dying with pain.

For this reason Monday burns like oil
at the sight of me arriving with my jail-face,
and it howls in passing like a wounded wheel,
and walks like hot blood toward nightfall.

And it shoves me along to certain corners, to certain damp
     houses,
to hospitals where the bones stick out of the windows,
to certain cobblers' shops smelling of vinegar,
to streets horrendous as crevices.

There are birds the color of sulfur, and horrible intestines
hanging from the doors of the houses which I hate,
there are forgotten sets of teeth in a coffee-pot,
there are mirrors
which should have wept with shame and horror,
there are umbrellas all over the place, and poisons, and navels.

I stride along with calm, with eyes, with shoes,
with fury, with forgetfulness,
I pass, I cross offices and stores full of orthopedic appliances,
and courtyards hung with clothes hanging from a wire:
underpants, towels and shirts which weep
slow dirty tears.

1959

WIDOWER'S TANGO

Pablo Neruda   Spanish   1904–

Oh Maligna, by now you will have found the letter, by now
    you will have cried with rage
and you will have insulted the memory of my mother
calling her a rotten bitch and a mother of dogs,
by now you will have drunk alone, all by yourself, your
    afternoon tea
with your eyes on my old shoes which are empty forever,
and by now you will not be able to recall my illnesses, my
    dreams at night, my meals
without cursing me out loud as though I were still there,
complaining of the tropics, of the *coolies corringhis,*
of the poisonous fevers which were so hard on me,
and of the horrendous English whom I still hate.

Maligna, the truth of it, how huge the night is, how lonely the
    earth!
I have gone back again to single bedrooms,
to cold lunches in restaurants, and I
drop my pants and my shirts on the floor as I used to,
there are no hangers in my room, and nobody's pictures are on
    the walls.
How much of the shadow that is in my soul I would give to have
    you back;
the names of the months sound to me like threats
and the word winter is like the sound of a lugubrious drum.

Later on you will find buried near the cocoanut tree
the knife which I hid there for fear you would kill me,
and now suddenly I would be glad to smell its kitchen steel
used to the weight of your hand and the luster of your foot:

under the dampness of the ground, among the deaf roots,
in all the languages of men only the poor will know your name,
and the dense earth does not understand your name
made of impenetrable divine substances.

Thus it hurts me to think of the clear day of your legs
in repose like waters of the sun made to stay in place,
and the swallow that lives in your eyes sleeping and flying,
and the mad dog that you harbor in your heart,
and thus also I see the dead who are between us and will be from
    now on,
and I breathe ash and utter ruin in the air itself,
and the vast solitary space that will be around me forever.

I would give this wind off the giant sea for your hoarse breathing
heard in the long nights unmixed with oblivion,
becoming part of the atmosphere as the whip becomes part of
    the horse's skin.
And to hear you make water, in the darkness, at the bottom of
    the house,
as though you were pouring a slow, tremulous, silvery,
    obstinate honey,
how many times over would I yield up this choir of shadows
    which I possess,
and the clash of useless swords which is audible in my soul,
and the dove of blood, alone on my forehead,
calling to things which have vanished, to beings who have
    vanished,
to substances incomprehensibly inseparable and lost.

1959

DEATH ALONE

Pablo Neruda   Spanish   1904–

There are cemeteries all by themselves,
tombs full of soundless bones,
the heart going through a tunnel,
in darkness, in darkness, in darkness,
we die inward like a shipwreck,
like a strangling of the heart,
like falling away from the skin of the soul.

There are cadavers,
there are cold sticky slabs that are feet,
there is death in the bones
like a pure sound,
like a barking without a dog,
coming from certain fields, from certain tombs,
growing in the darkness like a lament or the rain.

Sometimes when I am alone I see
coffins with sails
weigh anchor with pale corpses aboard, women with dead
    braids,
bakers white as angels,
pensive girls married to notaries,
coffins ascending the vertical river of the dead,
the purple river,
toward the source, their sails filled with the sound of death,
filled with the silent sound of death.

Death comes to the sonorous
like a shoe without a foot, like a suit without a man,
it comes to knock with a ring without a stone and without a

finger,
it comes to shout without a mouth, without a tongue, without
    a throat.

Nevertheless its footsteps resound
and its garments resound, silently, like a tree.

I do not know, I have little learning, I can scarcely see,
but I believe that its song is the color of moist violets,
of violets that are used to the earth,
for the face of death is green,
and the glance of death is green,
with the sharp moisture of a violet leaf
and its grave color of exasperated winter.

But death goes through the world also dressed as a broom,
it licks the ground looking for the dead,
death is in the broom,
it is the tongue of death looking for the dead,
it is the needle of death looking for the thread.

Death is in the little beds,
in the slow mattresses, in the black blankets,
it lives stretched out, and suddenly it breathes:
it breathes a dark sound which fills the sheets,
and there are beds navigating in a harbor
where death is waiting, dressed as an admiral.

1959

ODE WITH A LAMENT

Pablo Neruda   Spanish   1904–

Oh girl among the roses, oh pressure of doves,
oh garrison of fish and rose-bushes,
your soul is a bottle full of dry salt
and a bell full of grapes is your skin.

What a pity that I have nothing to give you except
the nails of my fingers, or eyelashes, or pianos melted by love,
or dreams which pour from my heart in torrents,
dreams covered with dust, which gallop like black riders,
dreams full of velocities and misfortunes.

I can love you only with kisses and poppies,
with garlands wet with rain,
my eyes full of ash-colored horses and yellow dogs.
I can love you only with waves on the shoulder,
amid random blows of sulfur, and waters lost in thought,
swimming against the cemeteries which run in certain rivers
with wet grass growing over the sad plaster tombs,
swimming across the sunken hearts
and the small pale pages of unburied children.

There is a great deal of death, there are funeral events
in my helpless passions and desolate kisses,
there is the water which falls in my head,
while my hair grows,
a water like time, a black unchained water,
with a nocturnal voice, with the cry
of a bird in the rain, with an unending
shadow, a shadow of a wet wing which protects my bones:
while I'm plain to be seen, while

I stare at myself endlessly in the mirrors and window-panes,
I hear someone following me, calling me, sobbing,
with a sad voice rotted by time.

You are standing over the earth, full
of teeth and lightning.
You propagate kisses and you kill the ants.
You weep tears of health, of the onion, of the bee,
of the burning alphabet.
You are like a sword, blue and green,
and you undulate to the touch like a river.

Come to my soul dressed in white, with a branch
of bleeding roses and goblets of ashes,
come with an apple and a horse,
for there is a dark room with a broken candelabra,
a few twisted chairs waiting for winter,
and a dead dove, with a number.

1959

AUTUMN RETURNS

Pablo Neruda   Spanish   1904–

A day dressed in mourning falls from the bells
like a fluttering veil of a roving widow,
it is a color, a dream
of cherries sunk in the earth,
a tail of smoke restlessly arriving
to change the color of water and of kisses.

I am not sure that it understands me: when night
approaches from the heights, when the solitary poet
at his window hears the galloping horse of autumn
and the trampled leaves of fear rustle in his arteries,
there is something over the sky, like the tongue of an ox,
thick, something uncertain in the sky and the atmosphere.

Things return to their place,
the indispensable lawyer, the hands, the oil,
the bottles,
all the signs of life: the beds, above all,
are filled with a bloody liquid,
the people deposit their secrets in sordid ears,
the assassins come down stairs,
but it's not that, but the old gallop,
the horse of old autumn, which trembles and endures.

The horse of old autumn has a red beard
and the froth of fear covers his cheeks
and the air which follows him is shaped like an ocean
and smells of vague buried decay.

Every day a color like ashes drops from the sky;
the doves must divide it for the earth:
the rope which is woven by oblivion and tears,
time which has slept long years in the bells,
everything,
the worn-out clothes, the women watching the snow fall,
the black poppies which no one can look at without dying,
everything falls into the hands which I raise
into the midst of the rain.

1959

WALTZ

Pablo Neruda   Spanish   1904–

I touch hatred like a daily breast;
I without ceasing come from garment to garment,
sleeping at a distance.

I am not, I do not serve, I do not know
anyone; I have no weapons of ocean or wood,
I do not live in this house.

My mouth is full of night and water.
The abiding moon determines
what I do not have.

What I have is in the midst of the waves.
A ray of water, a day for myself,
an iron depth.

There is no cross-tide, there is no shield and no costume,
there is no special solution too deep to be sounded,
no vicious eyelid.

I live suddenly and other times I follow.
I touch a face suddenly and murder myself.
I have no time.

Do not look for me then running over
the usual wild thread or the
bleeding net.

Do not call me: that is my occupation.
Do not ask my name or my condition.
Leave me in the middle of my own moon
in my wounded ground.

1959

THEY COME FOR THE ISLANDS
(1493)

Pablo Neruda   Spanish   1904–

The butchers laid waste the islands.
Guanahani was the first
in that history of torments.
The children of clay saw their
smiles smashed, battered
their stance slight as deers',
all the way to death they did not understand.
They were trussed up and tortured,
they were lit and burned
they were gnawed and buried.
And when time danced around again
waltzing among the palms
the green hall was empty.

   Nothing was left but bones
   rigidly fastened
   in the form of a cross, to the greater
   glory of God and of men.

   From the chief clay-pits
   and green boughs of Sotavento
   to the coral cays
   the knife of Narvaez went carving.
   Here the cross, here the rosary,
   here the Virgin of the Stake.
   Glowing Cuba, Columbus's jewel,
   received the standard and the knees
   in its wet sand.

         1968

MEMORIES OF YOUTH

Nicanor Parra   Spanish   1914–

All I'm sure of is that I kept going back and forth,
Sometimes I bumped into trees,
Bumped into beggars,
I forced my way through a thicket of chairs and tables,
With my soul on a thread I watched the great leaves fall.
But the whole thing was useless,
At every turn I sank deeper into a sort of jelly;
People laughed at my fits,
The characters stirred in their armchairs like seaweed moved by
    the waves
And women gave me horrid looks
Dragging me up, dragging me down,
Making me cry and laugh against my will.

All this evoked in me a feeling of nausea
And a storm of incoherent sentences,
Threats, insults, pointless curses,
Also certain exhausting pelvic motions,
Macabre dances, that left me
Short of breath
Unable to raise my head for days,
For nights.

I kept going back and forth, that's true,
My soul drifted through the streets
Calling for help, begging for a little tenderness,
With pencil and paper I went into cemeteries
Determined not to be fooled.
I went round and round the same fact,
I studied everything in minute detail
Or I tore out my hair in a tantrum.

And in this state I began my classroom career.
I heaved myself around literary gatherings like a man with a
     bullet wound.
Crossing the thresholds of private houses,
With my sharp tongue I tried to get the spectators to understand
     me,
They went on reading the paper
Or disappeared behind a taxi.
Then where could I go!
At that hour the shops were shut;
I thought of a slice of onion I'd seen during dinner
And of the abyss that separates us from the other abysses.

1965

THE TUNNEL

Nicanor Parra   *Spanish*   *1914–*

In my youth I lived for a time in the house of some aunts
On the heels of the death of a gentleman with whom they had
    been intimately connected
Whose ghost tormented them without pity
Making life intolerable for them.

At the beginning I ignored their telegrams
And their letters composed in the language of another day,
Larded with mythological allusions
And proper names that meant nothing to me
Some referring to sages of antiquity
Or minor medieval philosophers
Or merely to neighbors of theirs.

To give up the university just like that
And break off the joys of a life of pleasure,
To put a stop to it all
In order to placate the caprices of three hysterical old women
Riddled with every kind of personal difficulty,
This, to a person of my character, seemed
An uninspiring prospect,
A brainless idea.

Four years, just the same, I lived in The Tunnel
In the company of those frightening old ladies,
Four years of uninterrupted torture
Morning, noon, and night.
The delightful hours that I had spent under the trees
Were duly replaced by weeks of revulsion,
Months of anguish, which I did my best to disguise

For fear of attracting their curiosity.
They stretched into years of ruin and misery.
For centuries my soul was imprisoned
In a bottle of drinking water!

My spiritualist conception of the world
Left me obviously inferior to every fact I was faced with:
I saw everything through a prism
In the depths of which the images of my aunts intertwined like
    living threads
Forming a sort of impenetrable chain-mail
Which hurt my eyes making them more and more useless.

A young man of scanty means can't size things up.
He lives in a bell jar called Art
Or Pleasure or Science
Trying to make contact with a world of relationships
That only exist for him and a small group of friends.

Under the influence of a sort of water vapor
That found its way through the floor of the room
Flooding the atmosphere till it blotted out everything
I spent the nights at my work table
Absorbed in practicing automatic writing.

But why rake deeper into this wretched affair?
Those old women led me on disgracefully
With their false promises, with their weird fantasies,
With their cleverly performed sufferings.
They managed to keep me enmeshed for years
Making me feel obliged to work for them, though it was never
    said:
Agricultural labors,
Purchase and sale of cattle,
Until one night, looking through the keyhole
I noticed that one of my aunts—

The paralytic!—
Was getting about beautifully on the tips of her toes,
And I came to, knowing I'd been bewitched.

1965

THE VIPER

Nicanor Parra   Spanish   1914–

For years I was doomed to worship a contemptible woman,
Sacrifice myself for her, endure endless humiliations and sneers,
Work night and day to feed her and clothe her,
Perform several crimes, commit several misdemeanours,
Practice petty burglary by moonlight,
Forge compromising documents,
For fear of a scornful glance from her bewitching eyes.
During brief phases of understanding we used to meet in parks
And have ourselves photographed together driving a
    motorboat,
Or we would go to a nightclub
And fling ourselves into an orgy of dancing
That went on until well after dawn.
For years I was under the spell of that woman.
She used to appear in my office completely naked
And perform contortions that defy the imagination,
Simply to draw my poor soul into her orbit
And above all to wring from me my last penny.
She absolutely forbade me to have anything to do with my
    family.
To get rid of my friends this viper made free with defamatory
    libels
Which she published in a newspaper she owned.
Passionate to the point of delirium, she never let up for an instant,
Commanding me to kiss her on the mouth
And to reply at once to her silly questions
Concerning, among other things, eternity and the after-life,
Subjects which upset me terribly,
Producing buzzing in my ears, recurrent nausea, sudden fainting
    spells,

Which she turned to account with that practical turn of mind
    that distinguished her,
Putting her clothes on without wasting a moment
And clearing out of my apartment, leaving me flat.

This situation dragged on for five years and more.
There were periods when we lived together in a round room
In a plush district near the cemetery, sharing the rent.
(Some nights we had to interrupt our honeymoon
To cope with the rats that streamed in through the window).

The viper kept a meticulous account book
In which she noted every penny I borrowed from her,
She would not let me use the toothbrush I had given her myself,
And she accused me of having ruined her youth:
With her eyes flashing fire she threatened to take me to court
And make me pay part of the debt within a reasonable period
Since she needed the money to go on with her studies.
Then I had to take to the street and live on public charity,
Sleeping on park benches
Where the police found me time and again, dying,
Among the first leaves of autumn.
Fortunately that state of affairs went no further,
For one time—and again I was in a park,
Posing for a photographer—
A pair of delicious feminine hands suddenly covered my eyes
While a voice that I loved asked me who am I.
You are my love, I answered serenely.
My angel! she said nervously.
Let me sit on your knees once again!
It was then that I was able to ponder the fact that she was now
    wearing brief tights.
It was a memorable meeting, though full of discordant notes.
I have bought a plot of land not far from the slaughterhouse,
    she exclaimed.
I plan to build a sort of pyramid there

Where we can spend the rest of our days.
I have finished my studies, I have been accepted to the bar,
I have a tidy bit of capital at my disposal;
Let's go into some lucrative business, we two, my love, she
  added,
Let's build our nest far from the world.
Enough of your foolishness, I answered, I have no confidence in
  your plans.
Bear in mind that my real wife
Can at any moment leave both of us in the most frightful
  poverty.
My children are grown up, time has elapsed,
I feel utterly exhausted, let me have a minute's rest,
Get me a little water, woman,
Get me something to eat from somewhere,
I'm starving,
I can't work for you any more,
It's all over between us.

1965

THE TRAP

Nicanor Parra   Spanish   1914–

During that time I kept out of circumstances that were too full
    of mystery
As people with stomach ailments avoid heavy meals,
I preferred to stay at home inquiring into certain questions
Concerning the propagation of spiders,
To which end I would shut myself up in the garden
And not show myself in public until late at night;
Or else, in shirt-sleeves, defiant,
I would hurl angry glances at the moon,
Trying to get rid of those bilious fancies
That cling like polyps to the human soul.
When I was alone I was completely self-possessed,
I went back and forth fully conscious of my actions
Or I would stretch out among the planks of the cellar
And dream, think up ways and means, resolve little emergency
    problems.
It was at that moment that I put into practice my famous method
    for interpreting dreams
Which consists in doing violence to myself and then imagining
    what I would like,
Conjuring up scenes that I had worked out beforehand with the
    help of powers from other worlds.
In this manner I was able to obtain priceless information
Concerning a string of anxieties that afflict our being:
Foreign travel, erotic disorders, religious complexes.
But all precautions were inadequate,
Because, for reasons hard to set forth
I began sliding automatically down a sort of inclined plane.
My soul lost altitude like a punctured balloon,
The instinct of self-preservation stopped functioning

And, deprived of my most essential prejudices,
I fell unavoidably into the telephone trap
Which sucks in everything around it, like a vacuum,
And with trembling hands I dialed that accursed number
Which even now I repeat automatically in my sleep.
Uncertainty and misery filled the seconds that followed,
While I, like a skeleton standing before that table from hell
Covered with yellow cretonne,
Waited for an answer from the other end of the world,
The other half of my being, imprisoned in a pit.
Those intermittent telephone noises
Worked on me like a dentist's drill,
They sank into my soul like needles shot from the sky
Until, when the moment itself arrived
I started to sweat and to stammer feverishly,
My tongue like a veal steak
Obtruded between my being and her who was listening,
Like those black curtains that separate us from the dead.
I never wanted to conduct those over-intimate conversations
Which I myself provoked, just the same, in my stupid way,
My voice thick with desire, and electrically charged.
Hearing myself called by my first name
In that tone of forced familiarity
Filled me with a vague discomfort,
With anguished localized disturbances which I contrived to
    keep in check
With a hurried system of questions and answers
Which roused in her a state of pseudo-erotic effervescence
That eventually affected me as well
With incipient erections and a feeling of doom.
Then I'd make myself laugh and as a result fall into a state of
    mental prostration.
Those ridiculous little chats went on for hours
Until the lady who ran the pension appeared behind the screen
Brutally breaking off our stupid idyll.
Those contortions of a petitioner at the gates of heaven

And those catastrophes which so wore down my spirit
Did not stop altogether when I hung up
For usually we had agreed
To meet next day in a soda fountain
Or at the door of a church whose name I prefer to forget.

1965

ON THIS EARTH

Blas de Otero   Spanish   1916–

What kills me
is my
chest.

(Chest
shaped like
Spain.)

Get lots of air, the doctor
told me, lots of ai—

—OK, where?

1959

MY FRIEND ALWAYS . . .

Claudio Rodriguez   Spanish   1934–

Not he who in spring goes out to the field
and loses himself in the blue festivities
of men whom he loves, and is blind to the old
leather beneath the fresh down, shall be my friend always

but you, true friendship, celestial pedestrian, who in winter
leave your house in the breaking dawn and set out
on foot, and in our cold find eternal shelter
and in our deep drought the voice of the harvests.

1958

KINAXIXI

Agostinho Neto   Portuguese   Angola   1922–

I liked to sit down
on a bench in Kinaxixi
at six o'clock of a hot evening
and just sit there . . .

Someone would come
maybe
to sit beside me

And I would see the black faces of the people
going uptown
in no hurry
expressing absence in the jumbled Kimbundu
they conversed in.

I would see the tired footsteps
of the servants whose fathers also are servants
looking for love here, glory there, wanting
something more than drunkeness in every alcohol

Neither happiness nor hate

After the sun had set
lights would be turned on and I
would wander off
thinking that our life after all is simple
too simple
for anyone who is tired and still has to walk.

1962

NIGHT

Agostinho Neto   Portuguese   Angola   1922–

I live
in the dark quarters of the world
without light or life.

Anxious to live,
I walk in the streets
feeling my way,
leaning into my shapeless dreams,
stumbling into servitude.

———Dark quarters,
    worlds of misery

where the will is watered down
and men
are confused with things.

I walk, lurching
through the unlit
unknown streets crowded
with mystery and terror,
I, arm in arm with ghosts.

And the night too is dark.

1962

FRIEND MUSSUNDA

Agostinho Neto   Portuguese   Angola   1922–

Here I am,
friend Mussunda,
   Here I am,

with you.
With the established victory of your joy
and of your conscience.

     ——you whom the god of death has made!
     you whom the god of death has made, made . . .*

Remember?

The sadness of those days
when we were there
with mangoes to eat,
bemoaning our fate
and the women of Funda,
our songs of lamentation,
our despairs,
the clouds in our eyes,
Remember?

Here I am,
friend Mussunda.

---

*These two lines, in the native language of Angola, are part of a children's chant.

To you
I owe my life,
to the same devotion, the same love
with which you saved me
from the constrictor's embrace

to your strength
which transforms the fates of men.

To you,
friend Mussunda, I owe my life to you.

And I write
poems you don't understand!
Can you imagine my anguish?

Here I am,
friend Mussunda,
writing poems you don't understand.

It wasn't this
that we wanted, I know that,
but in the mind, in the intelligence,
that's where we're alive.

We're alive,
friend Mussunda,
we're alive!

Inseparable
still on the road to our vision.

The hearts beat
rhythms of foggy nights,
the feet dance

the sounds do not die in our ears

——*you whom the god of death has made* . . .

We're alive!

1962

TO POPE JULIUS II

Michelangelo   Italian   1475–1564

Sir if one of the old proverbs
is true it's *He who can will not*
You have been taken in by little stories
words
and have rewarded the enemies of truth

I was faithful to you long ago and have not changed
As rays are given to the sun I gave you
myself
but my days are nothing to you
never touch you
the more I try the less I delight you

Once I hoped to be raised by your eminence
know your massive justice and the might of your sword
when I needed them
not the voice of echo

But heaven itself mocks any virtue that looks
for a place in the world
sending it to pick fruit from a dry tree

1967

Happy the man who like Ulysses
  has made a good voyage or like him who seized
  the fleece and then came back knowing and wise
  to spend among his kin the rest of his days

Alas when will I see smoke from the chimneys
  of my little village and in what season look
  on the walled garden of my simple house
  that is a province and much more to me

I would rather have the roof my fathers made
  than the proud fronts of Roman palaces
  and thin slate rather than their hard marble

rather the Gaulish Loire than Latin Tiber
  my little hill than the Mount Palatine
  the sweetness of Anjou than the wind from the sea

1967

DEDICATION OF A MIRROR

Jean Antoine de Baïf   French   1532–1589

I that for letting a smile's favor
Loose from my youth in a light hour
Would with suitors' press and fervor
Find my doorway darkened over
Now to Venus for her to keep
The promised mirror tender up,
For the shape which of late I wear
Is such as will not bear review
And the face once this surface knew
Stirs no such shadows any more.

1948

INSCRIPTION FOR A FOUNTAIN

François de Malherbe   French   1558–1628

Passer-by, see how this water
Wells up and away is whirled:
Thus flows the glory of the world.
Only God remains forever.

1958

I'D RATHER DRINK

Michel-Jean Sedaine   French   1719–1797   song published in 1784

Let Saladin the emperor
In his garden bring together
A whole flock of damsels, all
Young and all delectable,
For his after-breakfast pleasure;
    Never mind, never mind,
That's quite harmless, to my mind;
I'm like Gregory: I think
    I'd rather drink.

Let a lord or lofty noble
Pawn the tower of his castle
To depart for the crusade,
Let him leave his lady bride
In the hands of worthy people;
    Never mind, never mind,
That's quite harmless, to my mind;
I'm like Gregory: I think
    I'd rather drink.

Let Richard, when his courage calls,
Brave a multitude of perils
So that, far from England, he
May subdue another country
Full of heathen infidels;
    Never mind, never mind,
That's quite harmless, to my mind;
I'm like Gregory: I think
    I'd rather drink.

1957

ROMANCE OF JOSEPH

Alexandre Duval   French   1767–1842   song published in 1821

Fourteen years I knew at most,
Scarcely from infancy removed,
When I followed in my trust
Those wicked brothers whom I loved.
Our numerous flocks we left to graze
Upon green Sichem's pasture-lands.
Still simple as a child I was,
And timid even as my lambs.

Close by three palms that stood alone
Unto the Lord I said my prayer,
When, by those wicked brothers taken . . .
I tremble even now with fear!
Into a damp and cold abyss
They thrust me down with angry force,
While I against their crime oppose
Only my innocence and tears.

Alas, when I was near to die
They brought me forth out of that grave.
To merchants from Arabia
They tendered me, to be a slave.
While they the price paid for their brother
Counted, and shared out the gold,
I, alas, wept for my father
And the ingrates who had me sold.

1957

LETTER FROM MEXICO

Tristan Corbière   French   1845–1875

VERA CRUZ, FEBRUARY 10TH

You gave me the boy to look after.—He's dead.
And more than one of his mates too, poor dear creature.
The crew . . . there's no crew any more. Maybe one or
　　Two of us will get back. That's the luck of it.

Nothing's as grand as that: a Sailor—ask any man;
What they all want to be, on land—That's sure enough.
Without the discomfort. And it's nothing else: look what a
　　tough
　　Apprenticeship, and he'd only begun!

I cry writing it down, I, old *Weather-Eyes*.
I'd have given my own skin, yes I would, like that,
To send him back to you . . . It's not my fault. It's not.
　　It makes no sense, that sickness.

The fever strikes like bells here. We'll all be
Drawing our rations in the cemetery.
The zouave calls it—he's from Paris, that one—
　　'*The garden of acclimatization.*'

Console yourself. They're all dying like flies. I found
A couple of things in his bag, keepsakes: a picture
Of a girl, and a pair of slippers, small size, and
　　Marked: *Present for my sister.*

He said tell his mamma he said his prayer.
Tell his father he would rather have fallen
In a battle. Two angels were with him at the end.
  A sailor. An old soldier.

1958

PARIS AT NIGHT

Tristan Corbière   French   1845–1875

IT IS NOT A CITY, IT IS A WORLD.

—It is the sea—flat calm—and the spring tide,
With the thunderings far out, has departed.
It will be back, the swell, in its own sound rolling.
—Listen to that: the crabs of night at their scratching . . .

—It is the dry bed of the Styx: Diogenes,
That rag-man, lantern in hand, calm as you please,
Passes. By the black stream perverted poets
Fish, using their empty skulls for worm-pots.

—It is the field: a flight of hideous harpies,
Wheeling, pounces to glean scabby bandages;
The gutter-rabbit, out after rats, keeps wide
Of Bondy's boys, who tread their grapes by night.

—It is death: the police sleep.—Above, love
Has her siesta, sucking the meat of a heavy
Arm where the dead kiss raises its red sign . . .
The single hour.—Listen: not a dream moving.

—It is life: listen: the living spring sings
The everlasting song on the slobbering
Head of a sea-god stretching his green limbs and naked
On a morgue slab, with his eyes open wide.

1958

THE MIRABEAU BRIDGE

Guillaume Apollinaire   French   1880–1918

Under the Mirabeau Bridge the Seine
Flows and our love
Must I be reminded again
How joy came always after pain

Night comes the hour is rung
The days go I remain

Hands within hands we stand face to face
While underneath
The bridge of our arms passes
The loose wave of our gazing which is endless

Night comes the hour is rung
The days go I remain

Love slips away like this water flowing
Love slips away
How slow life is in its going
And hope is so violent a thing

Night comes the hour is rung
The days go I remain

The days pass the weeks pass and are gone
Neither time that is gone
Nor love ever returns again
Under the Mirabeau Bridge flows the Seine

Night comes the hour is rung
The days go I remain

1956

AUTUMN

Guillaume Apollinaire   French   1880–1918

A bow-legged peasant and his ox receding
Through the mist slowly through the mist of autumn
Which hides the shabby and sordid villages

And out there as he goes the peasant is singing
A song of love and infidelity
About a ring and a heart which someone is breaking

Oh the autumn the autumn has been the death of summer
In the mist there are two gray shapes receding

1956

STAR

Guillaume Apollinaire   French   1880–1918

I think of Gaspard that certainly was not
His real name he is travelling he has left the town
Of Blue Lanchi where all the children called him papa
At the foot of the calm gulf facing the seven islands
Gaspard walks on and longs for the rice and the tea
      The milky way
At night since naturally he is walking
Only at night often catches his eye
      But Gaspard
Knows full well that one must not follow it

1956

THE TIP OF THE FLAME

Jules Supervielle   French   1884–1960

All through his life
He had liked to read
By a candle
And often he passed
His hand over the flame
To convince himself
That he was alive,
That he was alive.

Since the day he died
He has kept beside him
A lighted candle
But he hides his hands.

1960

REPOSE IN CALAMITY

Henri Michaux   French   1899–

Calamity, my great laborer,
Sit down, Calamity,
Take it easy,
Let's take it easy for a minute, both of us,
Easy.
You find me, you get the hang of me, you try me out,
I'm the ruin of you.

My big theater, my harbor, my hearth,
My golden cave,
My future, my real mother, my horizon,
In your light, in your great spaces, in your horror,
I let myself go.

1962

MY LIFE

Henri Michaux   French   1899–

You go off without me, my life,
You roll,
And me, I'm still waiting to take the first step.
You take the battle somewhere else,
Deserting me.
I've never followed you.

I can't really make out anything in your offers.
The little I want, you never bring it.
I miss it; that's why I lay claim to so much.
To so many things, to infinity almost . . .
Because of that little bit that's missing, that you never bring.

1962

SIGNS

Jean Follain French 1903–

Sometimes when a customer in a shadowy restaurant
is shelling an almond
a hand comes to rest on his narrow shoulder
he hesitates to finish his glass
the forest in the distance is resting under its snows
the sturdy waitress has turned pale
he will have to let the winter night fall
has she not often seen
on the last page
of a book of modest learning
the word end printed
in ornate capitals?

1960

THE PLATE

Jean Follain   French   *1903–*

When the serving girl's hands
drop the pale plate
the color of clouds
the pieces have to be picked up
while the light trembles overhead
in the masters' dining room
and the old school stammers
an uncertain mythology
in which one hears the names
when the wind stops
of all the false gods.

1967

EVE

Jean Follain   French   1903–

One book has it that Eve
came from the haya root
meaning live
and at the same time creatures
sure of their existence
pass on to girls knowledge
of human passions
but the youngest
holds a blond apple
on a hollow sill
and does nothing else
before she sleeps.

1967

EXILE

Jean Follain   French   1903–

In the evening they listen to the same
music no one could call gay
a face appears at the corner
of the inhabited world
the roses open
a bell has rung under the clouds
in front of the posts of the doorway.
A seated man says to all comers
in his gray velvet
showing his furrowed hands
as long as I live no one
touches my dogs my friends.

1967

IMPERIAL HAMLET

Jean Follain French 1903–

In the hamlet in the rye fields
they still live in a manner
becoming to ceremony
the doors stand open.
The word liberty
engraved in a stone
is reflected in a broken mirror.
The roots of a tree
stand out of the scuffed ground.
One of the houses
has two lamps
someone who lives there is putting on
a garment lined in scarlet
from the days of his youth.

1967

SOLITARIES

Jean Follain   French   1903–

Their doors always open badly
behind them the fire-colored
animal is asleep
they know whoever passes
on the curving road
man or women just by the footstep
they watch for a moment
the ornate lamp
hanging from the black ceiling
a spotted green plant dying
mourns for a lost child
under the vast low sky
then at last it snows.

1967

WORLD'S END

Jean Follain   French   1903–

At the world's end
on worn-out ground
the one talks of the flowers
adorning Argonne china
in their red pigment is mixed
the gold of old Dutch ducats
dissolved in aqua regia.
How quickly the night falls
the other answers
as things have it
in this shapeless country.

1967

NOCTURNAL HEART

Anne-Marie Kegels   French

Master of blood I am yours.
O tireless captain
upright on the plains of sand,
at night, at night I hear you
march toward a doubtful sea
with footsteps falsely restrained
—at that time I touch my breath,
I search for you with my bare wrist,
I defend you against the seaweed,
the salt, the wakened fish,
we faint under a wave,
people tell of two that are drowned,
of a fog mowing the beach.

Midnight descends, covers my lips,
keeps me from calling for help.
We float, forgotten by day.

1961

Pierre Delisle   French   1908–

Consider for a moment
The wakening of the minerals
To their omnipotence
When they will come
At night into the villages
And ambush the squeals of the unweaned
And steal their names.

1967

Voice closed like a lamp
The mother of memory
Says:

I give you my daughter
I give you memory

You will both be lost
You will both be absent

As long as she lives with you.

1967

Pierre Delisle   French   1908–

I love to speak in a low voice of the seasons of suffering.
They are she-asses travelling on the mountain
Looking for oblivion.

Children climb on their backs as they are seen to do in the parks
     of great houses
Then we stand for a long time with our chests against the grille
Our eyes become the past.

1967

A sowing of tears
on the changed face,
the glittering season
of rivers gone wild:
grief that hollows the earth

Age watches the snow
receding on the mountains

1967

DAWN

Philippe Jaccottet   French   1925–

Hour when the moon mists over
at the approach of a mouth
murmuring a hidden name

so that one can scarcely make out
the comb and the hair

1967

Every wing in the world had fallen.
The white snow lay still, glittering.
No cloud hung in the stars' pavilion.
No wave hammered the hard lake.

The lake's tree came up out of the depths
Till its top froze in the ice.
The lake spirit climbed up the branches
And looked hard through the green ice, upwards.

I stood on the thin glass there
That divided the black depths from me;
I saw, limb by limb, her beauty
Pressed close under my feet.

Through muffled sobbing her hands
Played over the hard lid.
I have not forgotten that lightless face;
It rises in my mind without end, without end.

1967

AT THE CASTING
OF THE THIRD SKIN

Friedrich Nietzsche   German   1844–1900

Now the skin on me warps and splits
and already the snake in me
has digested so much earth that it craves
for earth with a new heaving
and I crawl between stone and grass
hungering on my crooked way
to eat what I always ate you you
provender of snakes oh earth

1967

AGAINST THE LAWS

Friedrich Nietzsche   German   1844–1900

Starting now the hours of the clock
will hang on a hair around my neck
starting now the stars will stop
in their courses sun cock-crow shadows
and everything that time proclaimed
is now deaf and dumb and blind
for me all nature is silenced
with the ticking of the law and its measure

1967

My heart is standing up to its throat in yellow harvest light
   like land ripe for mowing under summer heavens.
Soon the song of the sickles will be ringing through the plain;
   my blood listens in the noon heat, sunk in happiness.
Granaries of my life, long desolate,
   all your gates will stand open like sluices;
the golden flood of sheaves will move on your floors like
   the sea.

1967

Look: the stars, the fangs
of light, and heaven and the sea,
what herdsmen's songs they
drive fading before them,
and you also who have summoned
voices and thought out your circle
follow the messenger
of night down the hushed steps.

Once you have emptied
the myths and the words, you must go,
you will not see again
a new company of gods,
their Euphrates thrones,
their writing, their wall—
pour, Myrmidon,
the dark wine on the land.

However the hours were welcomed,
anguish and tears of being,
everything blooms in the flowing
of this wine of night,
the aeon streams out in silence,
the shores have almost gone—
give back to the messenger
the crown, the dream, the gods.

1967

THE NIGHT FISHER

Johannes Bobrowski   German   1917–1965

In the beautiful foliage
the silence
unconsoled.
Light
with the hands
above a wall.
The sand flows from roots.
Sand
flow red in the water
far from here, follow
voices, make your way in the dark,
in the morning lay out your booty.
The voices pale as silver
sing.
Carry off to safety
in the beautiful foliage
the ears,
the voices sing: what
is dead is dead.

1967   translated with JEAN-PIERRE HAMMER

CICERO

Fedor Tyutchev   Russian   1803–1873

When the state tore at itself in agony
Rome's orator said, "I got up
too late and the night of Rome overtook me
on the way." Maybe,
but as you bade farewell to Rome's glory
you beheld from the Capitoline Hill
her bloody star
setting in full majesty.

Blessèd is he
whose visit to the world has fallen
in its moments of destiny.
The kind powers have welcomed him
to their banquet, to converse as an equal. He
sees the striding glories that they see,
he has a place at their councils, he drinks
from their own cup immortality,
in his time he lives as they do in heaven.

1968   translated with OLGA CARLISLE

TO ZINAIDA GIPPIUS

Alexander Blok   Russian   1880–1921

Those born in backwater years
forget their own way. Russia
gave birth to us in her years of anguish
and we can forget nothing.

Years of holocaust, do you
herald madness, or the advent of hope?
Days of war, days of freedom,
have stained our faces with bloody light.

We are speechless. The bells'
alarms sealed our lips. Where there was
a burning in our hearts once
there is nothing now, fixed, like a death.

Over the bed where we are dying
let the hoarse ravens sail—
may others, more worthy, O God, O God,
gaze on Thy kingdom!

1968   translated with OLGA CARLISLE

Wind whistles through the steep fence
    hides in the grass
a drunk and a thief
    I'll end my days
the light sinking in red hills
    shows me the path
I'm not the only one on it
    not the only one
plowed Russia stretches away
    grass and then snow
no matter what part I'd come from
    our cross is the same
I believe in my secret hour
    as in ikons not painted by hands
like a tramp who sleeps back of a fence
    it will rise my inviolate savior
but through the blue tattered fogs
    of unhallowed rivers
I may pass with a drunken smile
    never knowing him
no tear lighting up on my lashes
    to break my dream
joy like a blue dove
    dropping into the dark
sadness resuming
    its vindictive song
but may the wind on my grave
    dance like a peasant in spring

1967   translated with OLGA CARLISLE

In the country of yellow nettles
    the twig fences are brittle
the log houses huddle like orphans
    into the pussy-willows

through fields over the hills' blue
    by the greenness of lakes
a road of sand leads to the mountains
    of Siberia

Between Mongols and Finns Russia
    is lost there before she is frightened
along the road men make their way
    in irons

Each one has robbed or killed
    as his fate would have it
I am in love with the grief of their eyes
    and the graves in their cheeks

many have killed from pure joy
    they are simple-hearted
but in their darkened faces
    the blue mouths are twisted

I cherish one secret dream
    that I am pure in heart
but I too will cut a throat
    to the whistling of autumn

I too on the blown road
  on these same sands
will go with a rope at the neck
  to make love to mourning

I will smile as I go by
  I will swell out my chest
and the storm will lick over
  the way I came

1967 translated with OLGA CARLISLE

I am the last poet of the villages
the plank bridge lifts a plain song
I stand at a farewell service
birches swinging leaves like censers

The golden flame will burn down
in the candle of waxen flesh
and the moon a wooden clock
will caw caw my midnight

On the track in the blue field
soon the iron guest will appear
his black hand will seize
oats that the dawn sowed

In a lifeless and alien grip
my poems will die too
only nodding oats
will mourn for their old master

The wind will take up their neighing
they will all dance in the mourning
soon the moon a wooden clock
will caw caw my midnight

1967   translated with OLGA CARLISLE

It's done. I've left the home fields.
    There'll be no going back.
The green wings all over the poplars
    will never ring again.

Without me the hunched house sinks lower.
    My old dog died long ago.
I know God means I'm to die
    among the bent streets of Moscow.

I like the city, in its old script,
    though it's grown fat with age.
The gold somnolence of Asia
    dozes on the cupolas.

But at night when the moon shines, shines,
    shines, the devil knows how,
I take a side street, head down,
    into the same tavern.

A lair full of din and roaring,
    but all night till daylight
I read out poems to whores
    and drink with cut-throats.

My heart beats faster and faster,
    I pick the wrong moments
to say, "I'm like you, I'm lost,
    I can never go back."

Without me the hunched house sinks lower.
My old dog died long ago.
I know God means I'm to die
among the bent streets of Moscow.

1967   *translated with* OLGA CARLISLE

PRAYERS FOR THE FIRST
FORTY DAYS OF THE DEAD [3]

Sergey Esenin   Russian   1895–1925

Have you seen
running on the plain
on shoes of cast metal
the train hiding in the lake mists
blowing down its iron nostrils

and behind him
galloping over the high grasses
as though in the wild races at a fair
flinging his thin legs toward his chin the colt
with the red mane

the darling
the little idiot
where does he think he's running
Doesn't he know that all his kind
have lost to the steel cavalry
Doesn't he know there's no racing
in unnoticed fields that can bring back
the time when they'd trade
to the north of the Black Sea
for the right horse
two beautiful girls from the plain country
The fate of markets has troubled the face
of our still waters
waking them with the gnashing of iron Now
for a locomotive it would cost you tons
of the meat and skins of horses

1967   translated with OLGA CARLISLE

They are drinking here again brawling sobbing
to the amber woes of the accordion
they curse their luck and they hark back
to a Russia—a Moscow—of other days

For my part I duck my head
my eyes foundering in wine
rather than look fate in the face
I think of something else for a while

There is something that we have all lost forever
my dark blue May my pale blue June
that must be why the corpse smell
dogs this frantic carousal

Oh today's a great day for the Russians
the home-made vodka's flowing
and the noseless accordionist's singing
of the Volga and the secret police

They're grumbling that bony October
caught them all in its blizzard
courage has gone back to whetting
the knife from its boot

A hatred shifts in the eyes
rebellion grates in the raised voices
and they pity the young and foolish
whose blood flamed up and burned away

Where are you now and why so far
do we shine brightly for you
the accordionist's on a vodka cure
for his clap caught in the civil war

No the lost Russia will not be silenced
on all sides the rot feeds a wild courage—
oh Russia my Russia
rising in Asia

1967   translated with OLGA CARLISLE

I have forgotten the word I wanted to say.
A blind swallow returns to the palace of shadows
on clipped wings to flicker among the Transparent Ones.
In oblivion they are singing the night song.

No sound from the birds. No flowers on the immortelles.
The horses of night have transparent manes.
A little boat drifts on the dry river.
Among the crickets the word fades into oblivion.

And it rises slowly like a pavilion or a temple,
performs the madness of Antigone,
or falls at one's feet, a dead swallow,
with Stygian tenderness and a green branch.

Oh to bring back also the shyness of clairvoyant
fingers, the swelling joy of recognition.
I shrink from the wild grieving of the Muses,
from the mists, the ringing, the opening void.

It is given to mortals to love, to recognize,
to make sounds move to their fingers,
but I have forgotten what I wanted to say
and a bodiless thought returns to the palace of shadows.

The Transparent One still speaks, but of nothing.
Still a swallow, a friend known as a girl, Antigone.
The reverberations of Stygian remembrance
burn like black ice on one's lips.

1967   translated with OLGA CARLISLE

165

When Psyche, who is Life, steps down into the shadows,
the translucent wood, following Persephone,
a blind swallow casts itself at her feet
with Stygian tenderness and a green branch.

The shades swarm to welcome the refugee,
their new little companion, and greet her with eager wailing,
wringing their frail arms before her
in awe and trouble and shy hope.

One of them holds out a mirror, and another, perfume,
because the soul is a woman and fond of trifles.
And the silence of the leafless forest is spotted
with transparent voices, dry laments, like a fine rain.

And in the fond confusion, uncertain where to begin,
the soul does not recognize the transparent woods.
She breathes on the mirror and she still clutches
the copper wafer, the fee for the misty crossing.

1967   translated with OLGA CARLISLE

The thread of gold cordial flowed from the bottle
with such languor that the hostess found time to say
here in mournful Tauris where our fates have cast us
we are never bored—with a glance over her shoulder.

On all hands the rites of Bacchus, as though the whole world
held only guards and dogs. As you go you see no one.
And the placid days roll past like heavy barrels. Far off
in the ancient rooms there are voices. Can't make them out.
   Can't answer.

After tea we went out into the great brown garden.
Dark blinds are dropped like eyelashes on the windows.
We move along the white columns looking at grapes. Beyond
      them
airy glass has been poured over the drowsing mountains.

I said the grape vines live on like an antique battle,
with gnarled cavalry tangling in curving waves.
Here in stone-starred Tauris is an art of Hellas: here, rusted,
are the noble ranks of the golden acres.

Meanwhile silence stands in the white room like a spinning
      wheel,
smelling of vinegar, paint, wine cool from the cellar.
Do you remember in the Greek house the wife they all loved?
Not Helen. The other. And how long she embroidered?

Golden fleece, where are you then, golden fleece?
All the way the heaved weight of the sea rumbled.
Leaving his boat and its sea-wearied sails,
Odysseus returned, filled with space and time.

1967   translated with OLGA CARLISLE

I could not keep your hands in my own,
I failed the salt tender lips,
so I must wait now for dawn in the timbered Acropolis.
How I loathe the aging stockades and their tears.

The Achaeans are constructing the horse in the dark,
hacking out the sides with their dented saws.
Nothing quiets the blood's dry fever, and for you
there is no designation, no sound, no modelled likeness.

How did I dare to think you might come back?
Why did I tear myself from you before it was time?
The dark has not faded yet, nor the cock crowed,
nor the hot axe bitten wood.

Resin has seeped from the stockade like transparent tears
and the town is conscious of its own wooden ribs,
but blood has rushed to the stairs and started climbing
and in dreams three times men have seen the seductive image.

Where is Troy, the beloved? The royal, the queenly roof.
Priam's high bird house will be hurled down
while the arrows rattle like dry rain
and grow from the ground like shoots of a hazel.

The pin-prick of the last star vanishes without pain,
morning will tap at the shutter, a gray swallow,
and the slow day, like an ox that wakes on straw,
will lumber out from its long sleep to cross the rough haycocks.

1967   translated with OLGA CARLISLE

THE BLIND MUSICIANS

Iosip Brodsky   Russian   1940–

The blind go their way
    by night.
It's easier to cross
the squares
    at night.
The blind live
feeling their way,
brushing the world with their hands,
knowing neither shadow nor light,
and their hands drift over the stones
built into walls
of men, women,
children,
        money,
walls that cannot be broken,
        better
to follow along them.
Against them the music
        hurls itself
and the stones soak it up.
In them the music dies
under the hands.
It's hard dying at night, hard
to die feeling your way.

The way of the blind is
simpler, the blind
        cross the empty squares.

1967   translated with WLADIMIR WEIDLÉ

THE VERBS

Iosip Brodsky   Russian   1940–

In the silence the verbs surround me
like faces of strangers,
                    the verbs,
famished verbs, naked verbs,
essential verbs, deaf verbs,
verbs with no names, mere verbs,
verbs that live in caves,
speak in caves,
are born in caves,
under the shifting levels
of the universal optimism.

They go to work every morning,
mix cement, haul stones,
build the city . . . No, they erect
a monument to their own solitude.
They recede as we disappear in the memory
of someone else, they keep in step beside words,
and with their three tenses in line,
the verbs climb the hill Golgotha.

The sky is above them
like a bird above a cemetery.
They stand upright
as though in front of a closed door
and a man lifts his arm and drives nails
into the past
into the present
into the future.

No one will ever come to bear witness.
The strokes of the hammer
become the rhythm of eternity.
Under the verbs stretches the hyperbole, earth,
and heaven, the metaphor, drifts above them.

1967   translated with WLADIMIR WEIDLÉ

THE JEWISH CEMETERY

Iosip Brodsky   Russian   1940–

The Jewish Cemetery near Leningrad:
a lame fence of rotten planks
and lying behind it side by side
lawyers, businessmen, musicians, revolutionaries.

They sang for themselves,
got rich for themselves,
died for others.
But always paid their taxes first;
      heeded the constabulary,
and in this inescapably material world
studied the Talmud,
      remained idealists.
Maybe they saw something more,
maybe believed blindly.
In any case they taught their children
      tolerance. But
      obstinacy. They
sowed no wheat,
      never sowed wheat,
simply lay down in the earth
      like grain
and fell asleep forever.
Earth was heaped over them,
candles were lit for them,
and on their day of the dead raw voices of famished
old men, the cold at their throats,
shrieked at them, "Eternal peace!"
Which they have found
      in the disintegration of matter,

remembering nothing
forgetting nothing

behind the lame fence of rotten planks
four kilometers past the streetcar terminal.

1967   translated with WLADIMIR WEIDLÉ

174

THE MONUMENT

Iosip Brodsky   Russian   1940–

Let us set up a monument
in the city, at the end of the long avenue,
or at the center of the big square,
a monument
that will stand out against any background
because it will be
quite well built and very realistic.
Let us set up a monument
that will not disturb anybody.

We will plant flowers
around the pedestal
and with the permission of the city fathers
we will lay out a little garden
where our children
will blink
at the great orange sun
and take the figure perched above them
for a well-known thinker
a composer
or a general.

I guarantee that flowers will appear
every morning
on the pedestal.
Let us set up a monument
that will not disturb anybody.
Even taxi drivers
will admire its majestic silhouette.
The garden will be a place

for rendezvous.
Let us set up a monument,
we will pass under it
      hurrying on our way to work,
foreigners will have their pictures taken
      standing under it,
we will splash it at night with the glare
      of floodlights.

Let us set up a monument to The Lie.

1967   translated with WLADIMIR WEIDLÉ

W. S. MERWIN

W. S. Merwin was born in New York City in 1927 and grew up in Union City, N.J., and in Scranton, Pa. From 1949 to 1951 he worked as a tutor in France, Portugal, and Majorca. Since then he has made the greater part of his living by translating from French, Spanish, Latin, and Portuguese. In addition to poetry, he has written articles, chiefly for *The Nation*, and radio scripts for the BBC. He has lived in England, France, and the United States. His books of poetry are *A Mask for Janus* (1952), *The Dancing Bears* (1954), *Green with Beasts* (1956), *The Drunk in the Furnace* (1960), *The Moving Target* (1963), and *The Lice* (1967). His translations include *The Poem of the Cid* (1959), *Spanish Ballads* (1960), *The Satires of Persius* (1961), *Lazarillo de Tormes* (1962), and *The Song of Roland* (1963).